CAREERS IN
BASEBALL

BY HOWARD J. BLUMENTHAL

LITTLE, BROWN AND COMPANY

Boston   Toronto   London

Acknowledgments

I wish to thank the following people, who were instrumental in preparing this book:

Mark Andersen
John Cordova
Cathy Davis
Richard Deats
Ian Duff
Heather Ellmaker
Nancy Faust
Steve Frey
Stephen Green
Eric Gregg
Bill Larsen
Dennis Lehman
Ken Lehner
Steve Lehner
Leigh McDonald
Jay McLaughlin
Carrie Muskat
Sharon Pannozzo
Rick Rizzs
Terry Savarise
Susan Selig
Howard Starkman
Charles Steinberg
Mike Tatoian
Reggie Waller

Also, two very special thank-yous: first to Stewart Wolpin, who served as both baseball consultant and traveling companion; second to my good friend and brother, Bob Blumenthal, to whom this book is dedicated.

Copyright © 1993 by Howard J. Blumenthal

First Edition

All photographs were taken by Howard Blumenthal, with the exception of the following: (pp. 5, 13, 49) Courtesy Seattle Mariners; (p. 23) Courtesy Carrie Muskat; (pp. 72, 73) Courtesy Chicago White Sox; (p. 89) Courtesy Buffalo Bisons; (p. 121) Courtesy Baltimore Orioles; (p. 130) Courtesy Stewart Wolpin; (pp. 133, 136) Courtesy Cleveland Indians; (pp. 139, 147) Courtesy Montreal Expos; (p. 141) Donruss/Leaf, Inc.

Library of Congress Cataloging-in-Publication Data

Blumenthal, Howard J.
    You can do it! Careers in baseball / Howard J. Blumenthal.
      p. cm.
    Summary : An introduction to the variety of jobs available in baseball, on and off the field.
    ISBN 0-316-10095-1
    1. Baseball — Vocational guidance — Juvenile literature. 2. Sports personnel — Interviews — Juvenile literature. [1. Baseball — Vocational guidance. 2. Vocational guidance.] I. Title. II. Title: Careers in baseball.
    GV867.5.B58 1993
    796.357'023 — dc20   92-9542

10 9 8 7 6 5 4 3 2 1

HAL

Published simultaneously in Canada
by Little, Brown & Company (Canada) Limited

Printed in the United States of America

Contents

Introduction

Baseball is a complicated mixture of athletics, entertainment, marketing, warm summer nights, legends, statistics, fame and fortune, and, most important of all, dreams.

Thousands of people have jobs in baseball, most of whom are not players but just people who love the game and work behind the scenes. Some work at Yankee Stadium and Dodger Stadium and Comiskey Park; others work at Smith-Wills Stadium in Jackson, Mississippi; Pohlman Field in Beloit, Wisconsin; and McDermott Field in Idaho Falls, Idaho. Major league baseball players may get the headlines, but they're only a part of the whole. The baseball industry is a business with opportunities in all aspects of its organization and not only in the largest cities but in many of the smallest ones as well.

Take, for example, the Cleveland Indians. The overall direction of the organization is the job of the board of directors, a group of area businesspeople. The board appoints a president, just as in any company or business. In the case of the Indians, Hank Peters is the president. Hank concentrates on the playing aspects of the club: the players, the coaches, the managers, trading for or drafting new players, and competing against other teams. He leaves the day-to-day business operations to his senior vice president, Dennis Lehman, who supervises finances, accounting, public relations, community relations, ticket sales, stadium operations, the speakers' bureau, the ground crew, the clubhouse managers, and the office staff.

During the season, several hundred people work for the Cleveland Indians, including the front office staff, the players, and the temporary stadium staff (ushers, ticket sellers, and the medical staff, for example). During the off-season, the number drops below eighty.

It's wrong to assume that the Indians organization begins and ends at Cleveland Stadium. Like every major league team, the Indians are a national organization. The director of scouting employs an assistant and three regional scouting supervisors, one in West Palm Beach, Florida; another in Union City, Tennessee; and a third in Portland, Oregon. Additional senior-level scouts are based in Buffalo and Amityville, New York; Fruitland Park, Florida; and San Mateo, California. Two dozen more scouts are located throughout the country. Each is responsible for visiting high schools and colleges within a geographic area and reporting on players with major league potential.

Every major league team also operates a system of farm teams in various minor leagues. While some of these teams are owned by major league clubs, most are privately owned and operated. Each minor league club, or franchise, provides a stadium, a staff, and equipment. The major league team provides the players and decides which players will play at which minor league team and for how long. Minor league clubs compete in their own leagues; they have their own championship series and even their own league all-star games.

Players generally start in one of the rookie leagues. Cleveland's rookie league teams are the Burlington (North Carolina) Indians, who play in the Appalachian League, the Winter Haven Indians, who are in the Gulf Coast League, and the Watertown (New York) Indians, in the New York–Penn League. If a player shows promise, he moves up to a Class A league. The Kinston (North Carolina) Indians are the Cleveland Indians' Class A club; they play in the Carolina League. The next level up is Class AA; the Canton–Akron Indians, who play within driving distance of Cleveland, are in the Eastern League. Class AAA is one step below the major leagues. The Colorado Springs Sky Sox, Class AAA for the Cleveland Indians, play in the Pacific Coast League. Few players stay with a single organization from rookie league up to the majors; trading players from one organization to another has become common practice. The Indians also operate a spring training facility, Hi Corbett Field, in Tucson, Arizona.

If your talents lie in communications or public relations, consider the media and marketing jobs that are a crucial part of baseball. Each of the Cleveland area newspapers employs a reporter whose job, for more than half the year, is to cover the Indians. Staff is also required for radio and television coverage. Many companies work with the Indians to develop promotions that will encourage area residents to visit the stadium. Then there are the companies that produce major league baseball cards; they require photographers, statisticians, artists, printers, and salespeople to get the cards into retail stores. Several other companies have made a business of compiling baseball statistics for use by fans, teams, and the media.

Major League Baseball also operates several services for all of the teams in both leagues. Major League Baseball Productions, for example, produces television and home video programs, as well as promotional announcements. The Major League Players Association represents players in negotiations with team management.

Before you get too far into the book, consider your own career in baseball. How can you break into this industry? Read the newspapers — you may find a baseball professional in your neighborhood. That's how I connected with Montreal Expos pitcher Steve Frey — he lives about a mile from me. Or write some letters. My letters to the Phillies, the Cubs, and the White Sox yielded interviews with many of the people in this book. Or just call a minor league club. If you're lucky, and persistent, you'll get the right person on the phone and he or she will agree to meet you. That's how I ended up watching a wonderful game on a magnificent summer night, in a classic 1930s stadium by the Mississippi River in Quad City, Iowa.

Everyone in this book agreed to participate because they love baseball and because they want to help young people get into the industry. Listen to their advice. They know what they're talking about. ∎

Broadcaster
RICK RIZZS

W e were probably the most fortunate kids in town. Right behind our street was a field, about 150 feet wide, where we played baseball all summer long. We cut the grass; we manicured that field; we drew the baselines. We played baseball from sunup to sundown. I remember my mom calling me from the back door of our house. I'd always want to stay on the field, to finish the game."

Neighborhood baseball was Rick's life. "My friends and I pretended that we were major league stars. I was Luis Aparicio. My folks bought me a real White Sox uniform. That was one of my greatest childhood memories, playing in that field behind my house, being Luis Aparicio in that uniform.

"I saw my first major league game at Comiskey Park, and I'll never forget it. I remember coming into the stadium and seeing that explosion of green, all that grass and sunshine. I couldn't move. I was in awe. Then I saw the most incredible sight — the guy in the on-deck circle was number 7 for the Yankees, Mickey Mantle! I don't remember who won or lost, but every time I saw a pop-up, I thought it was going to be a home run. It was a big, big thrill."

By the time Rick was about fourteen, he still wanted to be a ballplayer, but he started to realize that many of his friends were more skillful. "I was a good little second

Rick Rizzs has broadcast games on radio for the Detroit Tigers and on radio and television for the Seattle Mariners.

baseman, a good fielder, but not doing a whole bunch of hitting." He played four years on the high school team.

"The first day of my junior year, Al Lokanc, my school's athletic director, called me into his office. He told me that I was going to be his student aide for the year. I sold tickets on game days, did some typing, and helped around the office. And one of my jobs was to announce for football games on the P.A. system. That led to a note from Chet Brown, the teacher in charge of the speech team; it turns out that there was a radio category. So I spent much of my junior and senior years preparing newscasts that I read in high school speech tournaments. I even won a few tournaments and went to the state championship.

"As a kid, I also used to imitate Jack Brickhouse, the Cubs' announcer. Now whenever I say, 'Good-bye, baseball' on a home run, which has become my signature, I think of Jack's 'Hey-hey' and his other mannerisms. I used to turn the sound down on the TV and pretend that I was Jack. I suppose I learned a lot that way."

It wasn't difficult for Rick to choose a college. "I wanted to go to Southern Illinois University because they had a great baseball program and I still wanted to play. But they also had a great communications program, including a television and a radio station where the students were allowed to do everything: directing, producing, working cameras. We all got a chance to find out what it was really like to do the job."

Rick was accepted at Southern Illinois. On the first day of baseball tryouts, he put on his sweats and spikes, walked about halfway to the field, saw about two hundred people already playing catch, and turned back. "I figured there was no way I was going to make that team. So I started walking back to the locker room and making plans to work just in broadcasting. But about halfway back, I stopped again. I said to myself, 'Hey, what am I doing? I'm quitting before I even start.' I decided to give it my best shot. In the next few weeks, I made it my business to be the first one on the field every day and the last one to leave. And I made the JV team in my freshman year."

Still, he didn't play much. "I learned a lot about baseball from the coach, Richard ('Itchy') Jones. He really knew how to teach the fundamentals." Rick spent half of his free time with the team and the other half at WSIU, the student radio station. He became a sportscaster for football and basketball.

WSIU did not broadcast baseball games — they were carried by the local ABC TV station, WCIL. Rick was working out with the varsity team in his junior year when WCIL offered him the sports director job. Part of the job was doing baseball play-by-play.

"I'll never forget my first day on the job. I was sitting up in the back of the bleachers with my friend Randy Jackson, who had done the first few innings. I was thinking about how much I missed being on the field in uniform, when he handed me the microphone. And all of the confidence that I had built up from playing in the field behind my house, all of the imitations of Jack Brickhouse, all of that came back to me. I just took off. I started talking baseball. At the end of the inning, Randy looked at me and said, 'It sounds like you've been doing this all your life!'"

Rick broadcast football, basketball, and baseball games for WCIL. He also became friendly with John Dittrich, a student who managed a video arcade near campus and worked part-time as a sports broadcaster at a local radio station. Dittrich got a job with Bobby Bragan, the president of the Texas League, and by the time Rick was ready to graduate, Dittrich was the general manager of the Alexandria (Louisiana) Aces, an AA club in the San Diego organization. As his graduation date grew near, Rick wrote to his friend John and asked him if any broadcasting jobs were available. "I didn't think anything would happen, because the season had started in April and I wasn't graduating until June."

Immediately after graduating, Rick packed everything he owned into his Ford Maverick and drove down to Tulsa to cover a

Lingo

Play-by-play:
Every radio and television broadcaster attempts to recreate the action and excitement of the game as he or she describes it to the audience. The play-by-play announcer describes exactly what is happening, step-by-step.

Press Box:
A large open office area where broadcasters and sports journalists watch the game. The press box is usually situated several levels up behind home plate.

Franchise:
Another word for a ball club. Major league baseball grants an exclusive contract to a business group to provide major league baseball games in a particular city or region. This contract is legally called a franchise agreement.

Stats:
Short for statistics, or more specifically, player statistics. Baseball is a game of numbers, where the percentage of hits versus the number of times at bat or the number of hits given up by a pitcher against a particular team are used to devise strategies.

Broadcaster

regional baseball tournament for Southern Illinois. On his way back to Chicago, he envisioned his next few weeks — visiting Chicago radio stations, sending out tapes to every team in the country, and getting lots of rejection letters. "I got home at about one in the morning, and my parents were still awake, so we got to talking. Then my mother said that some guy called from Louisiana. She didn't get his name, but she remembered him saying that the call could be returned anytime day or night. I figured it was John.

"I called John after 2:00 A.M. And he said, 'Rick, how would you like to come down to Alexandria, Louisiana? I already have a full-time radio announcer, but I'll let you do three innings of play-by-play if you'll be the visiting clubhouse manager.' I asked him what a clubhouse manager did, and he told me that I'd take care of the visiting club, that I'd wash their uniforms, shine their shoes, that sort of thing. I said okay and told him I'd be down in a few days. The job paid two hundred dollars a month. My dad thought I was crazy."

Rick's day began at 7:00 A.M. at the team's clubhouse, a small trailer with a little shower stall. He'd spend the morning scraping dirt off the team's shoes with a steel brush between doing washloads of laundry. At 1:00 P.M., he'd shower, put on clean clothes, and head into town to sell local merchants on promotions.

Savings and Loan Night was one promotion that kept him especially busy. There were four savings and loans in Alexandria, and they would purchase all of the seats in the ballpark. All the fans had to do was visit a bank, and they'd get a free ticket. "Putting together promotions like that was a major part of my job."

He'd hustle back to the ballpark by 4:00 P.M. to make sure that the clubhouse was ready for the players and that there were cold drinks and ice at hand. Then he'd run up to the press box to relieve the regular play-by-play announcer, Lynn Rollins, during the third, sixth, and seventh innings. After the eighth inning, Rick would run down to the clubhouse to take care of the visiting players. In addition to the two hundred dollars a month he was paid by the team, Rick earned fifty cents a day from each visiting player.

The next year, the franchise moved to Amarillo, Texas. Lynn Rollins decided to remain in Louisiana with his family, and Rick became the full-time radio voice of the Amarillo Gold Sox. Rick spent three years in Amarillo, learning all he could about the art of baseball announcing. Like hundreds of other minor league announcers, Rick daydreamed about working in the big leagues.

Rick's next job was also a result of his friendship with John Dittrich, who was now working with the National Association of Professional Baseball Leagues in St. Petersburg, Florida. At John's suggestion, the Memphis Chicks' general manager, Art Clarkson, called Rick. Art asked for a demo tape, a sample of Rick's work on the air. Rather than submitting an actual Gold Sox game, Rick went into a studio and recreated three innings of play-by-play, complete with sound effects for bat cracks, a cheering crowd, and even a sample commercial. Clarkson called back two days later to offer Rick the job. Rick was there within a week. Too busy to furnish his apartment, he slept on the floor until he found the time to settle in.

Three years later, Rick moved again, this time to WBNS radio in Columbus, Ohio. Now Rick was working for a station, not a ball team. He was the play-by-play announcer for the Columbus Clippers (the New York Yankees AAA team) and Ohio State football, and as sports director, he delivered sports news every morning as well.

"That was a tough schedule. I'd get to the station before 5:00 A.M. and do a minute-long sportscast every half hour. In between, I'd make calls and do interviews. I'd try to get home by noon. Then I'd take a nap for an hour or two, spend some time with my new son, and get out to the ballpark by 3:00 P.M. I'd spend the afternoon

"The job paid two hundred dollars a month. My dad thought I was crazy."

talking to the players and typing up my notes for the pre-game show and for my play-by-play. I'd get home by midnight — and wake up at about four in the morning to do the whole thing again the next day. I paid my dues. It was worth it, considering how far I've come."

Two years later, Rick had learned all he could in Columbus. Eight years in the business had provided him with enough training, he thought, to get a job in the major leagues.

"Throughout that winter, I sent tapes out to any club that might be looking for a broadcaster. It was after the season, but I was still on my afternoon nap schedule. One afternoon, my wife woke me up from my nap and told me that Melody Tucker, director of broadcasting for the Seattle Mariners, was on the phone. Melody told me that I was one of the finalists for a radio broadcasting job with the Mariners. I thought I was still asleep, that I was dreaming. Melody wouldn't tell me much more — when I asked how many other people were finalists and what it meant to be a finalist, she told me to call back in a week. Then she called right back to tell me that there were only five finalists. A few days later, she called to say that the list of finalists was down to two, that I was one of them, and that George Argyros, the owner, wanted to meet both of us. He was going to meet with the other guy first. By this time, I was a nervous wreck, but life goes on.

"Meanwhile, to celebrate the start of Girl Scout cookie season, the radio station had set up a celebrity cookie eating contest at a local mall. I managed to eat thirty-three cookies in just three minutes and finished third. The next morning, I thought I was having a heart attack. I raced to the hospital, and they took blood tests every eight hours — and all on the day when I was supposed to fly out to see George Argyros! By now we knew what had happened — I had eaten too many cookies — so I called Melody, and she started to laugh. A few days later, I flew out, met with George, and heard him say, 'Anybody who's willing to give his life for the Girl Scouts is okay by me!' Then he said, 'Welcome aboard.' I raced back to my hotel and called my folks, and they started crying. It was one of the best moments of my life."

But that's not the end of the story. After several years with the Mariners, Rick found out about a new opportunity. "In June 1991, I was in Detroit, talking to Ernie Harwell, the Hall of Fame broadcaster who had been with the Tigers for more than thirty years. We started talking about his situation, and I said, 'Ernie, I feel sorry for the guy who has to replace you when you retire.' He told me that I should apply for the job. It has always been my goal to be a number one announcer. When I got back to Seattle, I submitted a resume and tape." After a few interviews, Rick got the job as the number one radio broadcaster for the Tigers. "It's a great opportunity, a great team, great fans, a great ballpark. I'm going to love to go out there every day to do Tigers' baseball."

A Typical Day with the Mariners

"When we're home, I usually start the day by helping my son off to school. Then I read all of the available newspapers and take notes on what's happening throughout the league. That takes about three hours.

"To prepare for the game, I review my notes on both teams, paying particular attention to items that may be of interest to fans in the Pacific Northwest — how the team is doing, who's hot, what's happened in the past week, where the club stands in the league. Those details really matter."

If the team is away, then Rick spends an hour or two sightseeing, getting to know whatever American League city the Mariners happen to be visiting.

"I like to get to the ballpark early, say about 2:30 P.M. I spend some time with my partner, Dave Niehaus, and watch early batting

"A good 90 percent of the job is preparation."

practice. Then I go up to the press box, unpack my briefcase, and when the manager, Jim Lefebrve, has posted his lineups, I prepare notes about each player. Then I head down to the clubhouse and shoot the breeze with the players. We talk about last night's game, how things are going generally, how they're feeling. Basically, I'm chatting to get information that I can use on the broadcast."

Before the game, either Dave or Rick interviews Jim Lefebrve. The other does Mariner Watch, an interview with one or more players on either team.

"After we do the interviews, we talk to the other team's broadcasters. They're the ones who really know what's going on with their team. We also talk to players on the opposing team and to the manager. Then we head over to the dining room to chow down. Over the meal, we talk more baseball."

About an hour before game time, Rick goes back to the press booth. He reads through the player information and statistics provided by each team's public relations office, the stats from the American League, and his notes from the day's conversations.

"A good 90 percent of the job is preparation. There are so many times during the game when you have to fill in between the action. Radio provides the opportunity to paint a picture, to help people at home to imagine what's happening in the ballpark. I talk about the way the flag is blowing out in center field, how shadows are cutting across the field, about the Green Monster in left field at Fenway Park in Boston. Imagination plays a big part in radio."

Usually Rick starts the game on the radio side, doing the first two innings himself. At the top of the third, he changes over to TV and Dave goes to radio. Rick works television through the seventh inning. "I really have to gear down. I don't have to talk as much on TV because the cameras do so much storytelling. For example, I don't have to worry about calling every pitch. Instead, I concentrate on telling stories."

At the top of the eighth inning, Rick goes back to radio and Dave to TV. Joe Simpson stays on television, as the color analyst,

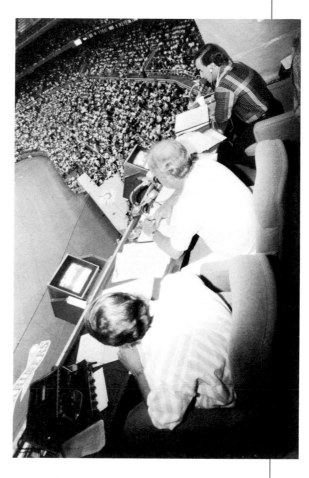

The view from the broadcast booth. By watching a game from high above home plate, Rick can see all of the action clearly.

for the whole game. By doing some radio and some television, the team gives the impression of having a larger broadcast staff — three broadcasters for television, two for radio — when, in fact, the five jobs are covered by just three people.

After the game, Rick and the other broadcasters get together to talk about the game. If the game is away, then it's back to the hotel or out with friends. If the game is in Seattle, Rick usually goes home. Baseball is important, but "the best times in my life are those that I spend with my wife, Kristi, and our son, Nick."

Rick's ADVICE

"Okay, you want to be a broadcaster. The next time you're watching a baseball game on TV, turn down the sound and do a little play-by-play." What else? Get out there and play lots of baseball.

By the time high school comes around, you'll probably have a sense of where you're headed, what you want to do. If your high school has a radio station, volunteer to be a broadcaster or to keep stats for a broadcaster. Read sports reports on the air. Or you could get in touch with a commercial radio station in your area and offer to cover high school sports. Tell them that you'll assemble scores and interview players and coaches. If you can't find a radio station that's close to home, work for a newspaper in the high school sports department. If you're persistent, someone will give you an opportunity. You probably won't get paid, but you will get a tremendous amount of useful experience.

"I'd choose a college where there's an active radio and television station, one where you can get hands-on experience. In addition, try to get involved with a local radio station in your college city or town. Go to a school that offers a wide variety of courses in journalism, television, and radio. Take lots of English courses, and do as much writing as possible. Having a good command of the language will make success more likely."

The best way to find your first job is to attend the winter baseball meetings, usually held in Florida, Arizona, or Hawaii. (For details, see the Where to Get More Information section of this book.) Invest in a plane ticket if you can, even if it's expensive. You will have the opportunity to meet people who work in the major and minor leagues. This is the place where the teams look for new employees — groundskeepers, salespeople, everything. It's possible to spend a few minutes talking to a minor league general manager, for example, to find out that the team needs a broadcaster or an assistant or a salesperson.

If you have access to a radio station, you can make a demo tape, complete with sound effects, to show your talent. Send a copy to every minor league team (you'll find their names and addresses in the Baseball America directory, which is listed in the Where to Get More Information section).

You might also get a job as an intern in a team's public relations office. If you're willing to work your way up through the ranks and be patient, you may get the opportunity. Many teams like to promote from within the organization. ∎

Computer Analyst
JAY McLAUGHLIN

S ince I went to school for computer science, I thought I would work for IBM or Hewlett-Packard, or for a big corporation in their computer applications group. But you know, it's funny: when I was young, whenever anyone asked me what I was going to do when I grew up, I always said that I was going to work for the Phillies."

Jay is the resident computer expert at the Phillies. He works in the baseball administration office, beside General Manager Lee Thomas, Director of Player Development Del Unser, Director of Scouting Jay Hankins, and Player Personnel Administrator Ed Wade. Just a few years out of college, Jay sits in on meetings that determine the fate of free agents or the strategies used in trading a player.

Jay doesn't make the decisions (though he hopes to be more involved in a few years). Instead, he provides detailed information that the team's executives use when making player decisions.

During the season, Jay attends every home game and keeps careful statistical records. He also makes one or two road trips each year. After each game, Jay enters the play-by-play data into the Phillies computer system: every hit, stolen base, balk, wild pitch, error, double play, every base

Jay McLaughlin compiles and analyzes player statistics for the Philadelphia Phillies.

hit pulled to left field — everything that might become valuable information later on. The stats are far more detailed than anything kept by fans: the Phillies' records of batted balls chart every baseball hit by the Phillies and their opponents — with the field broken down into 129 locations.

Jay writes his own computer programs and uses them to compile his statistical information and generate reports. He can tell you, for instance, which players are most likely to hit home runs while on the road, which outfielders are most likely to make errors on artificial turf, and which players hit well with runners in scoring position. Year round, he keeps an up-to-date roster on every team in the majors.

During the off-season, Jay prepares an end-of-season report that details each player's performance. This report is used for the Phillies' media guide and in contract negotiations.

"There is no easy way to measure a player's charisma or his power in bringing fans to the stadium. But statistics *can* be used to predict a player's value to the team. Can he add ten to fifteen wins per year? Is he a steady performer, or does he have good and bad years? Has he lived up to his potential? Is he at the prime of his career? The numbers may not tell the whole story, but they certainly provide an indication of how the player is doing and how he might fit into the team as a whole."

Jay is also involved in player development, keeping records of players in the Phillies' minor league system, adding reports from the Phillies' scouts, and accessing data from the Major League Baseball Scouting Bureau computers. All of this information is used to determine which players move up, which are traded, and which are added to the Phillies' organization. "I've also designed a program to help make decisions on the high school and college draft. It can identify, for example, a list of top shortstops. It can also sort by a lot of variables: shortstops who are good contact hitters with high fielding percentages and lots of range, for example."

There was a time when Jay wanted to be a ballplayer himself, when he was young and playing in Little League, but as he puts it, "I knew I was not a great athlete." He played sports for recreation, not competition. And mainly because they were his home team, he loved the Phillies.

"Baseball was my favorite sport, and I wanted to be involved in any way I could. That's why I became the student manager for my junior high school team. I kept the score book, the stats, and I was also the equipment manager. I reported the team's scores to the newspapers. I would have liked to be on the team, but I was only an average player. This way, I was able to stay involved in the game, but I also worked closely with the coach. I've always had rapport with both types of people."

In high school, Jay was the student manager of the baseball team for three years and worked in a similar capacity with the football team for two. "In my senior year, I also worked half days at the school athletic office, as part of a career study program. I typed schedules and contracts with umpires, kept the stats, and got to know what working in an office was like.

"My dad was an electrical engineer. He was always designing new devices and was deeply involved with computers at big corporations. So I was comfortable with the idea of computers. In fact, my high school was one of the first in the country with a program in computer science. Since I was good at math and science, I decided to take a computer course as an elective. Computers were, and still are, fun for me. I enjoyed the course and took a few more. I learned the basics of programming and even designed a program for the athletic department."

Jay's choice for college was the University of Delaware. "It was far enough from home so that I could live on campus, but it was close enough that I could go home whenever I wanted. I chose the school because it had a good athletic department, particularly baseball and football, and a good computer science program. I became a computer science major, but one of the first things I did

"I became a computer science major, but one of the first things I did when I arrived on campus was to visit the Sports Information Office."

when I arrived on campus was to visit the Sports Information Office. I trained for two years, and then, in my junior year, I became the baseball statistician. I also became the official scorer for football and kept stats for men's and women's basketball."

When Jay graduated, a friend's father set up an interview with IBM in Rochester, New York. Jay hoped he would get the job but had his doubts about moving to an unfamiliar city.

"Then, in mid-July, the baseball coach from the University of Delaware called me. Apparently, the Phillies had called several area schools — they were looking for someone with a background in baseball and in computers. They had been searching for a while. So I called them to request an interview."

Jay interviewed with the manager of information services and with the vice president of player administration. A week later, he was offered the job. But he didn't accept it right away.

"I still had the IBM job interview scheduled, and I didn't think it was right to cancel it, because my friend's father had gone to some trouble to set it up."

IBM offered him the job as well.

"It really wasn't a very difficult decision. The pay at the Phillies was not as good, but it was an opportunity to do what I wanted to do. I knew how hard it was to find a job in baseball, and I knew that if I waited, I might not get another offer or I might become too expensive to work in baseball." Also, the IBM job involved some work in sales as part of the training, and Jay was not interested in that.

"I've never worked anywhere else. I've been here for six years. The job hasn't changed, but the industry has changed a lot. The Phillies were once ahead of the other teams in the league as far as computers are concerned. Now the other teams are starting to catch up. Also, the computer industry is constantly changing, so there are always new projects. We're looking at our baseball information system and our internal network, so that the public relations people, and anyone else who needs statistics, can access

them directly from their own machines. And of course, I'm constantly updating and improving the programs — making them work faster, giving them more capabilities."

Jay eventually hopes to help make the player decisions, to offer more to management than just computer data. "I don't think I'd want to be negotiating with agents. Instead, I'd like to be a part of the group that takes a look at a new deal that, for example, the Angels, are proposing and comes up with a counterproposal. Still, computers are my niche, and I don't think I'd want to get too far away from them. But I would like to become more valuable from a baseball standpoint, eventually."

Jay's ADVICE

"You don't have to be a star athlete to be involved in baseball. If you really love the game, find yourself a niche, like I did."

Start by becoming a student of the game. Follow the players, the trades, and the stats. Read the newspaper's sports section every day. Read *Sporting News* and other baseball publications. Know what each player does well, who the important players are, and why. Keep stats on some players or teams. When you watch a game in person or on TV, figure out why the outfielders have shifted or why the third baseman is playing close to the base.

"If you're interested in computers, get some experience, either at school or at a friend's house or office. Learn what computers can do; learn about word processing and data base programs and spreadsheets. And spend as much time as you can on it — with computers, you learn by doing." Develop projects to help you learn. It's not hard to keep player stats by using a spreadsheet or data base program, for example.

In high school and college, work with the athletic department. Get some experience coaching Little League teams (in high school, you can coach eight- and nine-year-olds). Play if you can, but don't feel that you have to play in order to prepare for a career in baseball.

College will give you experience not only in school subjects but also in managing your time and developing your own life-style. "My college experience was valuable in a lot of different ways. One of the most important was learning to think more skillfully, and a lot of that came out of learning to program a computer.

"Finding your first job is never easy. I was lucky, but I was also prepared to take advantage of a good opportunity. Send out resumes, talk to everyone you know who might be able to help, and don't be afraid to accept a job that pays less than you had in mind."

Most of the opportunities in baseball are in the minor leagues, and if you're interested, try working with a AAA team. Minor leagues don't generally sign players, but they work with statistics, produce media guides, and can offer the opportunity to learn about public relations and marketing. If you know something about computers, for example, you might work with a minor league team to develop a ticket management system. But if you take a job like that, be forewarned that you're also going to pull the tarps over the field on a rainy day. It all comes with the job — in minor league teams, everyone does a little bit of everything. That's why they're a great place to learn and grow.

"Look for your niche. Work hard. Be patient. In time, you'll move up to the job you really want." ∎

Sports Reporter
CARRIE MUSKAT

Carrie Muskat covers baseball and other sports in the Chicago area for United Press International (UPI).

B eing a sportswriter is one of the most wonderful jobs in the world. I get paid to watch more than a hundred major league ball games a year. I have covered three All-Star Games and two World Series. I see players like Andre Dawson, Ryne Sandberg, Carlton Fisk, and Ozzie Guillen up close every day."

Carrie enjoys her work, but she also takes her responsibilities as a journalist seriously. "When I talk to the players, I'm working. I'm trying to get information to help me write a story. My job is to report on what is going on with the team. And to be able to report fairly, I have to keep my distance from the players. Let's say, for instance, that I became good friends with a shortstop, and one day he made a terrible play that cost his team the game. I would have to write about it — and I would have to be fair to my readers. That's a tough situation — which is why I don't recommend socializing with the players."

Carrie's original career plan had nothing to do with sports or baseball. "I was going to be a veterinarian — I was a little girl who loved horses. That was it — there was no changing me. Growing up in Glenview, Illinois, a Chicago suburb, I had a horse. His name was Horse (I guess I wasn't very creative)."

In a freak accident, Horse was hit by a car. The doctors could do nothing to save him. Carrie gave up her dream up becoming a vet and looked for another interest. She turned to sports. "I had always been a tomboy. One time, playing baseball in my front yard, I broke a window with a Wiffle ball."

Through high school, Carrie followed local teams in the *Chicago Tribune*'s sports pages. "I remember being amazed by the way that sportswriters told their stories. They were never boring. They were colorful, even poetic." Just for fun, Carrie took a journalism course during her senior year. Her first assignment was a news story. Since she had girlfriends on the swim team, she wrote about a swim meet. She found writing an easy task. "It was a way for me to be around my friends, so I started writing more stories about girls' interscholastic sports." The stories were published in the school newspaper. Then two weekly newspapers from Glenview called; they were looking for a reporter to write about girls' sports.

Carrie started writing a weekly column for the two suburban papers and continued her work for the high school paper. In less than a year, she had transformed a passing curiosity about sports journalism into a part-time job with a promising future.

For college, Carrie chose to go to Drake University in Des Moines, Iowa. "It was a small school with a wonderful journalism program. At some big schools, you have to wait until your junior year before you can take enough courses in your major to decide whether it's something you want to do." At Drake, Carrie could take journalism courses in her freshman year and see if the career was right for her. She picked magazine journalism as her major and pursued her interest in sports.

Carrie Muskat interviews manager Jeff Torborg.

Sports Reporter

23

"The paper wasn't sure what to do with a woman sportswriter. I was assigned to do a feature on putt-putt golf."

"I considered playing basketball for the Drake women's team. But during a preseason meeting, the coach told us how many stairs we'd have to climb every day in practice. I like hard work, but that sounded extreme. That's when I contacted the school newspaper office."

Carrie covered women's sports for the biweekly school paper, all the while dreaming about starting her own magazine. "I wanted to do a women's version of *Sports Illustrated*. Unfortunately, at about the same time, Billie Jean King came out with *Women's Sports* magazine, so that was the end of my idea." Undaunted, she created her own minor called Sociology of Sports and took a broad variety of courses, including Sports and the Law, and Group Behavior.

After her junior year, Carrie accepted an internship in the sports department at the *Cedar Rapids (Iowa) Gazette*. "The paper wasn't sure what to do with a woman sportswriter. I was assigned to do a feature on putt-putt golf. I worked the desk, which means answering phone calls from readers. I mainly covered high school summer sports like softball and American Legion baseball." Gus Schrader, then the sports editor, took Carrie to a minor league baseball game and taught her to keep a box score.

From that experience and others, she learned how important it is to understand the intricacies of the sports she writes about: "I learned more about the game of baseball during one women's softball tournament when I was named official scorer. To do that job, you must know the rules of the game — one of the scorer's duties is to decide when a player makes an error."

Carrie's strongest memory of the internship: "I learned how little time you actually spend at each event and how much research and desk work a sportswriter must do."

Back at Drake for her senior year, Carrie edited a city magazine and served as assistant sports editor for the school paper. She also worked part-time on Friday and Saturday nights at the *Des Moines*

Register, answering phones and preparing high school and college results from around the state. "I did a lot of what I call grunt work. I was willing to empty garbage cans just to be around a newspaper — to learn and get ahead. A lot of people were telling me that I'd never become a serious sports journalist, and a big part of the reason was because female sportswriters were so unusual. But I was stubborn. I knew what I wanted to do."

All of Carrie's work experience paid off. About three months after graduation, Carrie found a full-time job writing at the *Champaign (Illinois) Morning Courier.* "It was a Big Ten town — the University of Illinois is in Champaign — and there was plenty of action in the area high schools." She also learned to do layout: designing the newspaper's pages by arranging the stories, headlines, pictures, and advertisements. Unfortunately, the paper went out of business six months after Carrie arrived. "It happened during the girls' state high school basketball tournament. I remember typing the last story filed at the paper while everyone was packing up all around me."

To keep her mind off her joblessness, Carrie decided to go back to the tournament the next day and take some photos. She met a woman there who worked for United Press International (UPI). The woman knew that the wire service was looking for a sportswriter in the Des Moines bureau. Within a week, Carrie was working for UPI.

A sportswriter does not spend all of her time at the ballpark. "I ended up working the night shift for two years. Mainly I coordinated coverage of Big Ten and Big Eight sports and edited other reporters' stories. I also had to do a lot of newswriting. It was a great learning experience."

Carrie heard about an opening at UPI's Minneapolis bureau, applied for a transfer, and was accepted. In her new position, she would cover not only college but professional sports as well. "I was responsible for all of the sports news in the state. I covered

"I did a lot of what I call grunt work. I was willing to empty garbage cans just to be around a newspaper — to learn and get ahead."

everything — major league baseball, hockey, football, soccer, Big Ten sports, and high school state tournaments. But there was still a lot of desk work."

Carrie couldn't cover every event, so UPI paid stringers to go to some of the games. The stringers would call Carrie with information on how the teams played and scored. Then Carrie would write the story from the office. "I did cover a lot of major league baseball games myself. I was guided by one of UPI's veteran stringers, a man to whom I owe a lot, Bob Dodor."

Still, Carrie wanted a job in which she could cover sports in the field every day. She joined the *Rockford (Illinois) Register Star* as the sports columnist. Her timing was perfect. Gannett, the company that owned the paper, wanted to expand its baseball coverage. Because the *Register Star* was the Gannett paper nearest to Chicago, Carrie started writing about the Cubs and the White Sox.

"My work started appearing in *USA Today,* another paper owned by Gannett. They used my stories almost every day in 1989, when the Cubs clinched the National League East. Gannett owns newspapers all around the country, so my work ran in many other newspapers as well. I also covered the World Series that year, an experience I'll never forget because of the earthquake.

"Seeing my byline in other papers was great, but the best thing about my job at the Rockford paper was the chance to focus on baseball. When the editors asked me to change my beat, I decided to leave. I rejoined UPI in Chicago as a sportswriter.

"I am now one of UPI's top baseball writers. I covered the 1990 All-Star Game in Chicago and the American League Championship Series in Boston that year. I was assigned to three weeks of spring training in Florida in 1991 to do interviews with players, including Boston's Roger Clemens, Pittsburgh's Barry Bonds, St. Louis's Ozzie Smith, Baltimore's Glenn Davis, and Chicago's Tim Raines. Through the year, I cover the games."

"I am now one of UPI's top baseball writers."

During the off-season, Carrie switches to winter sports, including hockey, football, and basketball. "I covered the NBA finals in 1991 when the Chicago Bulls won. That was very exciting, but I couldn't wait to get back to baseball."

A UPI Reporter Covers a Game

"When the Cubs are in town, day games usually start at 1:20 P.M. I get to the ballpark at around 10:30 A.M. The first thing I do is check the lineup posted in the clubhouse. This information helps me prepare for interviews with the managers of both teams. I ask about injured players, pitching rotations, and for their thoughts on the previous game. I may also question them about trends — if the number of home runs is up around the league, for example. I also interview some of the players to get their opinions about their own performances and about the way that the team is competing.

"It's important to pay attention. Managers and players respect a well-informed reporter. I cut out the box scores from the newspaper and keep a scrapbook with every Cubs and White Sox game, home and away. That way, I can keep track of how a pitcher is doing or whether a hitter is in a hot or cold streak.

"If I don't know enough about the opposing team, I find a baseball writer who follows the team. When I talk to the opposing manager, I want him to feel I've done my homework, that I have kept up to date with his team. I'm constantly keeping track of statistics, injuries, and transactions.

"When the players begin batting practice, I observe. Batting practice is their time to work. I don't want to interrupt a ballplayer when he's taking his turn in the batting cage. White Sox hitting coach Walt Hriniak growls at anyone who interferes. Most players are very easygoing. But some sit and stare at their lockers before a game — they're not to be bothered. The starting pitcher also needs to be left alone, because he needs to concentrate on the game.

"Reporters are allowed on the field and in the clubhouse up to one hour before the game and immediately after it. We never go into the trainer's room or the players' lounge. The trainer's room is the players' sanctuary; some players escape reporters after a game by heading for the whirlpool. Andre Dawson doesn't hide, but we know he has a long treatment session for his knees before and after games. If we need to talk to him, we know we have to wait a long time in the clubhouse.

"After I've gathered some pre-game notes, I have a quick lunch in the cafeteria. The food is provided by the ball club, and it's more than just hot dogs and popcorn. Comiskey Park is well known for its Sunday brunch. I try never to miss a Sunday White Sox game.

"Then I head to my spot in the press box to transcribe my notes. For example, if Dawson isn't playing and the manager said it's because his knees are bothering him, I'll jot that down and add Dawson's average and how he has been playing lately. Each note runs about three or four paragraphs, and I try to write at least four items. The team also provides daily notes and statistical information. If two Cubs' outfielders are about to break the 100 RBI mark, the Cubs' notes would tell me the last time that two Cubs' outfielders drove in that many runs. The Cubs' notes also provide the pitching rotation for the current series and upcoming series. I file my notes before the game; they're sent to the newspapers and broadcasters who subscribe to UPI's service.

"Everyone in the press box has their own portable computer that hooks up to the telephone system through a modem. UPI's headquarters is in New York. When I file my stories, they appear in the New York computer system.

"I then fill in my lineup card, because I keep score during the game. I keep my score book neat and well organized so that I can use it for reference later on.

"My job with the wire service is to get the story out as soon as the game ends. I have to write a three-hundred-word story about the game before it's over. I concentrate on how the teams score. It's easiest for me to add to the story every time the team scores. Newspaper writers have a little more time, especially with day games. Their deadline is usually 10:00 P.M. My deadline is immediately after the final pitch, because we provide copy for broadcasters. Whenever you hear a radio announcer give you the highlights of the game, he or she got that story from a wire service.

"When there are six outs to go in the game, I send the story to New York using my portable computer. With three outs to go, I call the New York office. I stay on the line to make any changes and to report on the rest of the game. With 40,000 fans shouting in the background, you learn how to yell over the phone to the people in New York. And they yell right back.

"As soon as the game ends, I give the score once more to New York just to make sure that they have it right. Then I head to the clubhouse. I almost always talk to the manager first to get his impression of the game. I also talk to the winning pitcher, the losing pitcher, the game's hero, and any players involved in controversial plays. I want to get their description of what happened — how a pitcher felt, what pitches were working for him, if the home run was a surprise, if the sun got in a player's eyes when he missed catching the ball. These are not long, in-depth conversations because I have to file what we call an alternate lead, a rewritten version of the story's first paragraph, within an hour after the game ends. So in one hour, I have to interview players in both locker rooms, then get back upstairs to the press box and write a new story. I've learned to work fast.

"I've covered major league baseball since 1981, and I've learned to deal with the clubhouse. At first, being around players while they were undressing was uncomfortable. The players don't wait for reporters to leave before changing. They want to get out of their sweaty uniforms fast. There were times when players called me

Modem:
A device that connects one computer to another via telephone lines.

names or teased me in the clubhouse. But by now, the players accept me. Kirk Gibson used to be very difficult to deal with; he would scream at women reporters. But recently, when I was interviewing one of his Kansas City teammates who was not fully clothed, Gibson shouted at his teammates to leave me alone because I was a professional. He surprised me.

"Throughout my career, every time something bad happened involving the players, something great would happen the next day. I might be harassed one day, and the next, I'd watch a one-hitter or see a spectacular catch that saved the game. I still get goose bumps when I think of Gibson's game-winning pinch-hit home run in the 1988 World Series off Oakland's Dennis Eckersley. And I'll never forget how happy the Cubs were when they won the NL East in 1989. I was in Montreal to cover the division-clinching game and was doused with champagne. It's those thrills that make up for the long, long hours, the rain delays, the cold weather in the press box, and any problems in the clubhouse."

Trainer
MARK ANDERSEN

I work with Jeff Cooper, the Phillies' athletic trainer. Jeff is in charge of the department; he takes care of the administration, works with the team physician on serious medical problems, and works with players on specific rehabilitation programs. I'm the assistant trainer; I deal with the players on a day-to-day basis. Whatever a player needs, we give him. We tape ankles and give massages, whirlpool baths, and hot and cold packs. When players reach this level, they know what works for them."

Jeff spends much of his time in the training room. It's beside the clubhouse, where the players dress and relax before and after each game. The training room is filled with specialized sports medicine equipment. "We do whatever is necessary to keep the ballplayers in shape. If a player was previously injured, we tape his ankle before the game to make sure the problem doesn't come back. But there are times when a player asks us to tape his ankle because he feels he plays better that way. We're not there to question his judgment; if a player feels that way, he's probably right.

Mark Andersen is the assistant athletic trainer for the Philadelphia Phillies.

"We usually start our day at about 2:00 P.M. The first thing I do is fill the whirlpool bath; then I make sure we have enough supplies. If we're going to do a hot or cold treatment on a player with an injury, I set up for that. Right now, we're rehabbing a pulled muscle for one of our outfielders. For the first few days, we treated the muscle with an ice pack. Now we're starting on deep heat from our ultrasound machine. We also use an electric stimulator to work the muscle. Later, when the injury is healing, we might use the whirlpool. We usually massage the muscle as well."

Most of the players arrive at the stadium between 2:00 and 4:00 P.M., in time to work out and take batting practice. Individual players usually have their own exercise routines. Some prefer to stretch first, then visit the training room to have a wrist or knee taped up. Others visit the training room first; some don't visit the trainers unless they're having a specific problem.

"During batting practice, I get some time to work on record keeping in the training office. We keep a computer file on every player and log each injury. Each one has a code: 211R D 4, for example, means dislocated right thumb. We fill out injury reports on every player and send them to the manager, the general manager, and the president of the team. Our yearly report describes the injuries and what we did to correct them."

Dr. Marone, the team physician, arrives during batting practice. "We work closely with him and follow his orders for treatment." Dr. Marone is available to players throughout the afternoon and evening to discuss any medical matters.

Home batting practice for the Phillies ends at about 6:00 P.M. Then the opposing team takes its practice. In between batting practice and game time, Phillies players take care of their own business. The pitchers might have a meeting, for example, to discuss strategies to use against specific hitters on the other team. After the meeting, starters who are not scheduled to pitch that night might do some exercise on a bicycle or with weights. The relievers usually work out after the game.

Then the Phillies take infield practice. "During that practice, we concentrate on the starting pitcher. If he needs anything — a hot pack on his arm to get the blood flowing or a massage with heat, for example — we take care of his needs. He's the one who's going to be out there for us, and we make sure that he's in the best possible shape."

After fielding practice, some players ask for help from Mark and Jeff. "Some guys go out and play hard and don't ask for anything. And some guys enjoy a rubdown as part of their pre-game routine. If I taped someone up yesterday and he went 3 for 4, he'll probably come back to me and ask me to do it again for tonight's game."

A few minutes before game time, Mark packs up the medical kit and heads for the dugout. "The kit is a big box. Whatever we might need on the spot, it's in there." The kit has five drawers containing tape, scissors, ointments, all sorts of tools, and every variety of first-aid gear.

"Game time is usually our rest period. We watch from the bench in the dugout — at least one of us, either Jeff or I, is always sitting there, beside the players. If someone is hit by a pitch or hurt sliding, we can usually take care of the problem on the spot. But the action depends on the severity of the injury. Many times during the season, I drive to Methodist Hospital, which is ten blocks from the stadium, for X rays. We do this for the Phillies and for play-

"If someone is hit by a pitch or hurt sliding, we can usually take care of the problem on the spot."

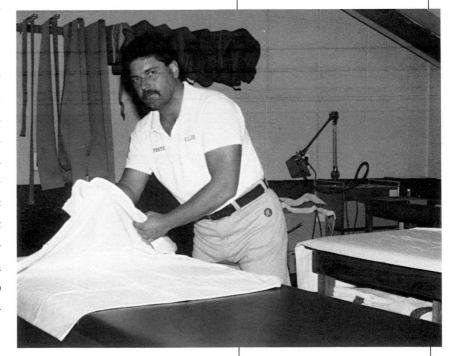

A baseball trainer must be equipped to handle a wide variety of minor injuries quickly and efficiently. All trainers pack a box of tools and supplies, which they carry to the dugout before every game.

Here's a brief list of items that most trainers provide in the dugout and on the field:
• Tapes and bandages in various widths and sizes
• Nonprescription pain-killers such as aspirin
• Creams and balms, for muscle pain
• Scissors, mainly to cut and remove bandages
• Eye black, to cut down on sun glare
• Massage oil
• Antibacterial ointment, for skin abrasions and small cuts
• Ice packs (not in the kit itself)
• Fluid-replacement drinks in large canisters

ers on the opposing team as well. When a pitcher leaves the game, we usually ice down his arm — pitching is not a natural motion, and the ice prevents inflammation."

After the game, Mark goes back to the training room and takes care of players' needs. "There are probably four guys who need ice packs after every game, from a previous knee injury, for example. They also come in here to talk about the game and hang out."

Jeff and Mark are usually in the training room until about an hour after the game. Then they shower and leave for home around midnight, sometimes later.

"We don't usually go out with the players, at least not socially. I'm on the Phillies staff, and I might know that someone is going to be traded. If the management knows that I'm close to that player, well, it would not be a good situation. We are friendly, but we try to keep things on a professional level."

Since Jeff and Mark travel with the team, they have few off-days during the season (remember: baseball teams work on weekends). Mostly, off-days follow tiring road trips, and Mark is pleased to have time off to spend with his wife.

The regular season ends by early October and does not begin again until six months later. Jeff and Mark's schedule lightens up a bit. Mark has an opportunity to work on his new house or enjoy sports such as hunting. But Jeff and Mark don't have six months off. Throughout the winter, they remain concerned about the players' well-being. "If a player is hurt, we'll try to find someplace in his hometown where he'll get good care." And by late December, they are making plans for spring training: ordering supplies, packing up everything they'll need for part of February and all of March in the Phillies' training center in Clearwater, Florida. Mark goes early; he works for two weeks at Dream Week, the Phillies' fantasy camp. "Spring training is when we really work long hours. We start at about 6:00 A.M. and work until dinnertime. Games are usually played in the afternoon."

Like many of the people who work for the Phillies, Mark grew up in the Philadelphia area. "In elementary school, I was a little overweight. I slimmed down by seventh grade, when I started playing football and wrestling. I got better every year. By ninth grade, I was a strong football player, but I broke my ankle, couldn't wrestle, and started falling behind. I didn't play in tenth grade because of the ankle. And in eleventh grade, I hurt my knee and ankle playing football — I was an offensive lineman.

"After I hurt my knee, I became aware of trainers. The trainer at my school who was rehabbing my knee taught me about the field. Since I wasn't really big or fast enough for college sports, I started thinking about teaching physical education or working as a trainer. I went to a state college and became certified to be a teacher. I also took courses in training and got my certification in the National Athletic Trainers Association, first as a student and then as a professional member."

While Mark was still in the eleventh grade, he started working part-time for the Phillies.

"I grew up in Abington, a suburb of Philadelphia. Kenny Bush, the team's clubhouse and equipment manager, lived in the area. He had children in the school system, and my mom knew him. The Phillies needed a bat boy, and he asked my mom if I might want the job. So I worked in the clubhouse in eleventh and twelfth grade as a bat boy. I kept at it for my first two years of college, too. All together, I worked there for five years, including the All-Star Game in 1976 and the World Series in 1980."

While Mark was a bat boy, the Phillies' athletic trainer, Don Seger, retired. His assistant, Jeff Cooper, moved up to become the trainer. And Jeff asked Mark to be his student trainer.

"Two years later, in 1983, I took my certification test and passed. And in 1984, I had my first job as a trainer, with the Spartanburg (South Carolina) Phillies, our A-level minor league team."

Lingo

Rehab:
Short for rehabilitation. After an injury, the player must heal and then gradually regain use of the injured muscle. In rehab, special exercises and other treatments may be required for complete recovery.

Ultrasound Machine:
A machine that uses sound waves to provide deep heat for injured muscles. (Another kind of ultrasound machine is used to show the inside of a body by creating an image on a monitor.)

Electric Stimulator:
A machine that stimulates muscles by delivering mild electric shocks.

Fantasy Camp:
A vacation in a baseball training facility, where amateurs can pay to play with former major league stars.

Mark wasn't just the team's trainer, however. "When you work in minor league ball, you're also the clubhouse manager, the equipment man, and the traveling secretary, sometimes booking flights and handing out meal money, calling hotels and pairing roommates."

In the fall of 1984, Mark was the trainer for the Phillies' instructional league. "They assemble all of the guys who need extra work, and they play in our Clearwater facility."

In 1985, Mark was the trainer for another Phillies A-level minor league team, the Peninsula Pilots in Hampton, Virginia. That winter, he got a job with a winter league club in Venezuela. "I contacted one of the Phillies' former coaches, Reuben Amaro. He knew I was interested in getting more experience and earning extra money during the off-season."

Finally, in 1986, Jeff Cooper asked Mark to become his full-time assistant trainer. "I didn't have to think about that for very long." Mark accepted the job, finished the season, spent another winter in Venezuela, got married, and settled into his present routine.

Eventually, he'd like to become a head athletic trainer. Chances are, Mark will leave Philadelphia when the right opportunity comes along. "With all of the expansion coming up, and more talk of it in the future, more jobs will become available and maybe one will come my way."

Mark's ADVICE

"The key word is persistence. You must keep at it. When I was in college, I remember very clearly that things were not going the way I thought they should. But everything works out if you keep your goals in sight and you're persistent about achieving them."

The best way to understand what trainers do is to learn all you can about sports, anatomy, first aid, CPR, and health in general. "I learned a lot through the Boy Scouts, the Y, and some lifesaving classes."

To get started, Mark suggests that you visit your school's athletic department. Let them know that you're interested in training. At many schools, you can be a student trainer. "Plan to spend most of your time watching and helping out. That's the best way to start. When I was in high school, I saw a poster of a trainer taping up someone's ankle, with a phone number to call to learn more about training. Most people just looked at the poster. But I took the time and trouble to make the phone call. Do the same. Show that you're interested, and you'll be far ahead of most people."

Mark also suggests becoming involved in team sports, either as a player or as a manager. "Learn how the team is organized and structured."

As for college, many schools offer degree programs in sports medicine and sports training. "You do not have to become a doctor. Trainers are not doctors." But it is important to take courses that will lead to certification in the National Athletic Trainers Association (2952 Stemmons Freeway, Dallas, TX 75247 — write for information).

Finding that first job is difficult. "It's tough to get in the door. Baseball is a big family. Working in the minor leagues is one way — the jobs are easier to find. Working in the clubhouse is another; those bat boy jobs are available. Let the team in your area know that you are interested and capable. And be *persistent!!*" It certainly helps if you know someone, but with the help of your parents, their friends, their friends' friends, your teachers, relatives, and friends from school, you should be able to find someone who knows a way in. And don't concentrate just on baseball. Experience in other sports is equally valuable. "There are a lot of minor league, high school, and college teams. If you're good, certified, and persistent, you will succeed."

Mark also suggests getting in touch with Cramer Products, a large manufacturer of sports medicines and training room equipment. They run student trainers' seminars, held in twenty-five to thirty college facilities throughout the United States. The seminars are designed for high school and college students with an interest in athletic training. Your high school's trainer should be able to provide details. You can also contact Cramer by calling 1-800-255-6621.■

Sports Photographer
STEPHEN GREEN

Stephen Green is the official team photographer for the Chicago Cubs.

Before the game today, I'm shooting baseball card pictures of the Giants — Matt Williams, Will Clark, and Kevin Mitchell — they're in town. Last night, Vice President Quayle and Senator Paul Simon were at the park, so I shot pictures of them for the Cubs archives. And I'm working on a series of photos that will be used to promote the Special Olympics. A few days ago, Pepsi sponsored a giveaway at the ballpark, and I shot a picture of one of the executives throwing out the first pitch. That's one of the most important aspects of my job — working with the marketing department on promotions. Photos for calendars, baseball cards, or newspapers and magazines are great, but it's the work with the marketing department that usually gets first priority."

Stephen Green has been the official team photographer for the Cubs for more than a decade. Unlike many of his peers, however, he did not work his way up from local newspapers or magazines. He was simply the right person for the job and came along at a time when the Cubs needed someone to fill the position.

"We had a darkroom in the basement, so I learned all about chemicals and developing when I was pretty young."

Stephen's story begins with his father, an amateur photographer. "He took pictures of our dog, of ships in the harbor, all the usual amateur stuff. We had a darkroom in the basement, so I learned all about chemicals and developing when I was pretty young." Stephen's dad worked in the media, producing public service spots at a Chicago advertising agency. "Watching my father work with clients taught me a lot about getting the job done, and done right. He also taught me how to set priorities at work, to satisfy several different masters while concentrating on my own work."

Stephen became interested in photography when he was about thirteen. "I used to spend hours looking through books of photographs and paintings. This wasn't all that I did, though. Mainly I was fantasizing about becoming a rock and roll star, or I was out playing sports or thinking about girls or wanting to drive a car. You know, normal stuff." He learned his way around his father's darkroom but never considered photography as a possible career. "This was something that I did just for fun. I wasn't serious enough even to shoot photos for the school paper. I just did it because I enjoyed it."

In college, at Evergreen State, a part of the University of Washington, Stephen became an art history major. Why so far from home? "I wanted to be someplace really beautiful. I had read about the state of Washington, and it sounded just right. Also, the school allowed me to create my own curriculum. I ended up spending a lot of time doing documentary photography, taking pictures of people at the Seattle Public Market, down by the wharves. After a year or so, I went to Europe, where I started meeting other students who were interested in photography. We started going to art galleries and museums together. It was a great learning experience." He adopted the European artist's life-style, drinking espresso, listening to Miles Davis, and admiring the work of two of the century's finest documentary photographers, Henri Cartier-Bresson and Alfred Eisenstadt. "Books of their work are widely available in libraries. They are essential study for anyone with even a passing interest in photography."

When he finished school, he moved to Portland, Oregon. He found a job as an assistant curator for the photography collection at the Portland Art Museum. In his spare time, he made photographs, at first for himself and eventually for *Portland* magazine. "I took pictures at cocktail parties, marathons, civic events — wherever I was needed. Then I found a job at a camera store, selling professional equipment. That's where I really learned about the proper tools, the right films to use, the right lenses. I think that's where I made the transition from amateur to professional photographer."

As Stephen's interest in photography grew, so did his list of heroes. "I discovered the whole Magnum Photos school, people like Brassaï and Robert Capa. Each of their photographs tells a story. They turned photojournalism into an art form. And again, anyone can see their work by just visiting a library. I started reading their biographies — I was really influenced by what they did and how they did it."

When the Portland economy took a downturn, Stephen found it difficult to earn a living. "People just weren't spending money on free-lance photography. I realized that I had to go to a bigger city. My choices were New York, Los Angeles, or Chicago. I liked living in Portland, but I missed a lot of the things that I enjoyed about Chicago — especially the blues clubs and watching baseball at Wrigley Field." He moved home to Chicago.

While seeking out clients for his free-lance business, Stephen waited tables at a Chicago restaurant. He also applied for several grants from foundations and government organizations that provide money to artists for projects of merit. The Illinois Arts Council approved a grant of five thousand dollars. "It was enough for me to live on for a few months. The grant was based on my proposal to take documentary photographs of a place that I've always loved: Wrigley Field. I had a year to complete it. I own the

"I took pictures at cocktail parties, marathons, civic events — wherever I was needed."

rights to the photos, but the Illinois Arts Council can display them in public buildings. I also sent a set to the Baseball Hall of Fame and another to the Library of Congress Photo Collection. Both have extensive archives that are used by researchers."

In order to create the Wrigley Field photographs, Stephen was in contact with the Chicago Cubs organization. After the project, as a result of new ownership, the Cubs found themselves in need of a new team photographer. "They had seen my work. They knew me — they knew that they could get along with me." Stephen was offered the job.

"This was a dream come true, the job of a lifetime. Everyone was so excited for me. I've been doing it for ten seasons now, and I love it. Dealing with the players is not always fun, and the pressure can get pretty intense because everyone has such high expectations and because the team has so many different needs. So I shuck and jive a lot, and try to give a little bit of my time to everyone who has a request."

Cubs publications are a priority. "I might have to get Andre Dawson in the batting cage for one publication, maybe a picture of someone selling popcorn for another."

For most games, the marketing department also has a long list of pictures that need to be made. "Let's say that it's Toyota tote bag day. The marketing department has five of the biggest dealers in the Midwest at the stadium, so I have to take pictures of each one in the dugout, in the on-deck circle, with a player, and with their name up on the scoreboard. And on the same day, we might be pitching IBM, so I have pictures to take for them as well. It takes some juggling, but I do my best to accommodate all of the requests.

"If I have a free-lance assignment for *Sports Illustrated* or *Sporting News* or *USA Today,* or a baseball card company, that's a lower priority. I get my own work done during the free moments between the Cubs' needs. Those published photos go to the newspapers or magazines, but they come back to the Cubs' archives, so the organization doesn't mind at all. Still, if everything is happening at once, things can get a little crazy. I set my own priorities, and I do my best to get everything done."

Stephen does most of his work before the game actually begins. During the game, he spends his time in the photo bay, on the outfield side of the dugout. "My needs are different from those of a newspaper or magazine photographer, who needs a great shot of every play. I may spend an entire game focusing on one player, looking for pictures that I can use in a calendar or yearbook or to illustrate a *Sports Illustrated* story on outfield defense. But the required skills are basically the same."

During a regular season game, the photo bay may be filled with a dozen photographers, each equipped with lenses that are two feet long. "We cooperate. We talk about when a particular player is likely to steal or bunt or whether he has any speed. We also compare notes on the best film and filters to use, because the light is different in every stadium. We trade a lot of technical information. Even though we're in competition for many of the same freelance jobs, we all help each other. It's a good way to learn and make better pictures."

A Professional Photographer at Work

Sports photography requires a combination of the right equipment and the right technique.

When Stephen works at Wrigley Field, he packs three Nikon cameras, each one equipped with a motor drive that can advance the film quickly enough to shoot five images per second. A 400- or 500-millimeter (mm) lens is long enough for action close-ups.

Monopod:
A one-legged camera support.

Exposure:
The amount of light that reaches the film. A picture that is overexposed is too light and may not show enough detail. A picture that is underexposed is too dark. When shooting in bright sunlight, it is a good idea to shoot with a low exposure to avoid letting in too much light and overexposing the image. Similarly, when shooting in relative darkness, adding exposure will improve the sharpness and number of details that can be seen in the photograph.

Converter:
A device that adds to the magnification power of a lens. It is a small tube that is attached to both the lens and the body of the camera.

Focal Length:

A measurement of a lens's magnification power. A lens with a long focal length provides more magnification than one with a shorter focal length. A 200mm lens provides ten times more magnification than a 20mm lens. Ten times magnification would make a person standing thirty feet away look as though he or she was standing just three feet away.

ASA:

Also called ISO, this is the speed of the film, a measure of how sensitive the film is to light. A film with an ASA of 64 is not as sensitive as a film with ASA 400. Films that are less sensitive usually show more true-to-life color. Higher speed films are useful when shooting action or when shooting in darker locations, but some picture quality may be lost.

Color Saturation:

The purity or strength of a color. Colors with less black, white, or gray are more fully saturated than colors that contain these neutrals.

For mid-range action, Stephen uses a 300mm lens. For candid player pictures and head shots, he prefers an 80 to 200mm zoom lens.

Stephen also brings a monopod to keep the camera steady; a tripod is too large for the photo bay and too cumbersome to carry around the stadium. A hand-held light meter allows more accurate exposures than the meter that's built into the camera body. A converter, placed between the body and the lens, doubles the focal length, effectively transforming a 500mm lens into a 1000mm lens with minimal loss of image quality.

He shoots slide film made by either Kodak or Fuji, with either 100, 200, or 400 ASA. "Slower films are a problem for action shots, and these films provide enough color saturation and clarity for newspaper or magazine publication."

At Candlestick Park, in San Francisco, and in other stadiums where the photo bay is farther away from the action, he brings a longer main lens, like a 600mm. And he prefers color negative film when shooting in an indoor location such as a domed stadium.

"Technique is the difference between an amateur and a professional. You have to know that the light in the outfield is different from the light at second base, and you have to learn to change the camera's settings in a split second, working more from instinct than anything else. All of this becomes second nature, but when you're starting out, you have to think through everything carefully.

"You must learn exposure, for example. A camera with automatic exposure may be okay if the light is flat, without extremes of sunlight or shadow. But what happens when you have a player with a light complexion wearing a dark uniform in a sunny outfield? You have to learn to expose the image properly so that the sun won't wash out the shot, so that both the uniform and the man's skin appear natural. It's a matter of taking control. The more pictures you take, the more you are able to control your

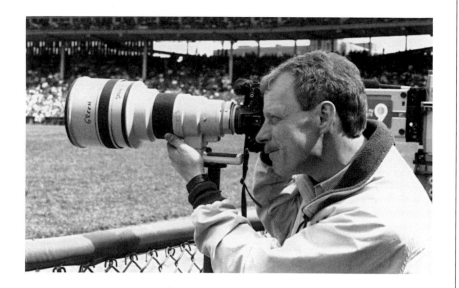

composition, your exposure, and of course, your focus. If any of these are less than perfect, the photo will not be accepted for publication."

The best way to start is to learn the game, so you can anticipate the action. This may allow an extra second to make the necessary camera adjustments. "Let's say that there's one man out, a runner on second, a left-handed pitcher, and a right-handed batter. If the pitcher has tremendous control, you're keeping an eye on that runner on second. But if the batter is Andre Dawson, you keep your eye on him because he might hit a home run. What's the likelihood of the first-base runner getting into a double-play situation? Does the right fielder have a great arm — could he throw someone out? If it's a Darryl Strawberry, his throw could mean a tag with the runner coming into third. You have to learn the game, to know the strategies, the players, how they are likely to react in any given situation. If that sounds like I'm saying that you've got to be a fan, that's probably right. The only difference is that I'm paid to be here every day."

Composition:
The arrangement of the items seen in a picture. Placing the subject in the center of the picture is safe, but not always imaginative. Placing the subject just off to the side, with a scoreboard or a dugout in the background, may result in a more interesting picture.

Portfolio:
A large folder that contains samples of a photographer's or artist's work. The portfolio is usually shown to employers in order to interest them in hiring a photographer for free-lance work.

Stephen's ADVICE

"Buy a good used manual camera so you can teach yourself the fundamentals of focus, composition, and exposure. I'd recommend a Nikon or a Canon so that you can get to know the systems, the lenses, and the different models made by these companies, because you'll be using either a Nikon or a Canon if you work professionally. Buy the longest lens you can — 300mm, 400mm, or even 500mm if you can find one. Don't buy a zoom; learn to shoot with a lens with a fixed focal length. If you can't afford to buy one, then rent one for weekends (that's one of the benefits of owning Canon or Nikon — lenses are widely available for rental).

"Next, start shooting pictures. Don't be inhibited. Everything you see is a possible subject. Don't just concentrate on one subject area such as sports. Take pictures of everything — anything that catches your eye. Go to a public library and look at other people's work. Teach yourself to find interesting details, to tell stories by composing the picture in a certain way. Take classes in photography, workshops — get whatever help you can. You may be surprised to find that there are plenty of photo instruction programs in your community. Then learn to develop your own pictures. You will understand more about light and exposure and what makes a good picture by making your own prints. It's not expensive to set up a home darkroom, especially if you're shooting in black-and-white.

"Once you're feeling confident about your work, volunteer to take pictures for your school yearbook or newspaper. If you're interested in sports, go to every game and shoot. You can cover your costs by selling the pictures to the players. Contact community newspapers and offer to trade your pictures for use of their darkroom. It's a great way to start a free-lance career."

At a certain point, you may feel as though you've reached a plateau. Your pictures are okay, but they don't look anything like the work in *Sports Illustrated*. What's wrong? You may not be getting in close enough. Can you arrange for permission to work closer to the action? Are you using a lens that's too short? Are there problems with exposure or composition, or do you need to take a course to improve your technique? The problem may also be the equipment you're using. Save some money and rent a professional setup for a weekend — a long lens, a motor drive, and enough film so that you can shoot without worrying about the cost of each image. "That's the best way to find out what's really going on." Do some research to find a professional sports photographer in your area. Write a nice letter, and you may be able to arrange for a short meeting to get a critique of your work.

As for college, it's not essential if all you want to do is shoot pictures. You could find yourself an apprenticeship with a pro, learn technique, get your portfolio together, and start calling on potential clients. Still, Stephen does recommend college. "College is a great place to learn technique, to compare notes with other student photographers, to critique one another's work, and to learn how to deal with people. Plus, it's fun to go to college. Most schools have darkrooms, equipment available to borrow at little or no charge, and places where you can get your work published or shown without the pressure associated with the real world.

"The way to get a job is to start working, first as a stringer for a local newspaper and then for larger clients. A college internship is a good way to make some contacts and to learn about the professional world. Minor league baseball is also a great place to master your skills, because conditions are professional but players are accessible. Women's sports is also a good place to begin, maybe to build an entire career on.

"The most important thing is that you want to take pictures, with or without the recognition, with or without the money. Those first few years can be frustrating if personal pleasure and the opportunity to learn are not enough to satisfy you. Eventually, the money and the recognition may come. And along the way, you may have the opportunity to go places and do things that other people only dream about — like watching a Major League All-Star Game from just beside the dugout, with a pass around your neck that guarantees pre-game access to the entire field and stadium and post-game access to the clubhouse." ■

Scout
REGGIE WALLER

Reggie Waller is the director of scouting for the San Diego Padres.

I am in charge of finding and signing amateur ballplayers for our minor league system. Basically, I coordinate the efforts of forty scouts, who work all over the United States and in Puerto Rico, Venezuela, the Dominican Republic, Canada, and Australia."

The emphasis of Reggie Waller's job is on scouting, but he has a background in player development as well. He started, as so many baseball professionals do, with a dream of playing pro ball.

"When I was about eleven, I was a very good student, but I really enjoyed athletics. I liked playing football better than baseball, but I never cared for football *practice*. I could practice baseball endlessly. I played shortstop, and I pitched. Being in the infield, where the best athletes were, I really had to learn the game. As an infielder, I was involved in just about every play, as a cutoff man, directing and communicating with the rest of the team. There are a lot of things that go by you if you're an outfielder; essentially, your job is to throw the ball to an infielder. That's why I encourage players to play in the middle of the diamond, specifically shortstop, second base, catcher, pitcher, and in addition, center field. When you play in the middle of the diamond, you're going to learn the game.

"I played Little League ball. I also played in our neighborhood league in southeastern San Diego, and I thought it was more fun than organized ball because there were no parents around. The kids in the neighborhood ran the league. We had about four or five kids on each team — we'd clear out a vacant lot, and we'd play. We even sold concessions. We had a regular organized schedule. The whole thing was supervised by Charlie Graham, a high school student who later played some college ball."

Reggie played in the Pony League when he was thirteen and fourteen. He realized that some of the guys who had played in his Little League, players who he thought had some ability, were not skillful enough to play in the Pony League. Reggie was starting to feel a little clumsy, but he was still more capable than many of the other boys. He also started playing alto saxophone. "I was a guy who went full-speed ahead into everything that interested me. I liked Motown music: the Temptations, Smokey Robinson, and I started playing that kind of music. I was also a good student; I enjoyed school."

Reggie was fortunate to attend Hoover High School. Hoover's baseball coach, Jerry Bartow, was considered the best in the city. "He was big on work ethic and on desire. He won a lot of games through the years. And if you were going to be a member of the baseball team, Bartow made sure that you got involved with the Key Club, a junior Kiwanis Club. That was the way we raised money for the baseball team — and because we were selling concessions at basketball and football games, we couldn't play other sports, so he kept our attention focused on baseball.

"By the time I was about sixteen, I started having some doubts about my ability to play professional ball. I've got twin boys who are going through the same situation now — my confidence disappeared with my coordination. Then my body weight started to catch up with me. One summer I grew five or six inches and gained about fifty pounds. My strength and coordination started coming back, but I hurt my knee working

"I was a guy who went full-speed ahead into everything that interested me."

at McDonald's. Still, I played JV and varsity baseball in high school. During the summers of my junior and senior years, I played in the American Legion league. The important thing, for me, was just to get into the lineup. I knew I was never going to be a big star. And I began to realize that I was not going to be a major league ballplayer."

Reggie went to San Diego Community College, and he played during his freshman and sophomore years there. "I wasn't the best player on my college team, but I was a good runner, I had some strength, and I had a good arm. The things that scouts look for, the things that I look for today, were there — even though the whole package wasn't there for me."

The next year, Reggie concentrated on building up his legs and getting into the best possible shape. He continued to play, and although he wasn't a star, he had what he calls "strong defensive ability, but lacking power."

"After my sophomore year in college, one of my friends needed a ride to Palomar Junior College in Escondido, where the Cincinnati Reds were running a tryout camp. My younger brother wanted to go, so I drove them both. I was convinced that I was not going to try out.

"When I got there, a local scout who worked out of the San Diego area saw me and asked why I wasn't dressed to work out. As it happened, I usually kept my baseball gear in my trunk. So I got dressed, and as I looked around, I started to realize, Hey, I can run better than this guy — I've got better range. It turned out to be one of the best days I ever had. Now I was getting excited again. But even more important, I was starting to understand what the scouts were looking for. Scouts don't look for the best fielder or hitter. They look for the best physical tools. That's why they ask you to throw a baseball from a certain distance or run the sixty-yard dash or field flies or ground balls. Apparently, I made the right impression. A week later, my brother and I saw our names in the paper. We had made the draft."

At that time, Reggie did not understand how the draft worked. Now he knows it inside and out. He explains: "A scout in the area gives the prospective player a score based on what he can do today and on what he projects the player will be able to do in the major leagues. If the player gets a high enough score, he's accepted for the draft. In the first round of the draft, each major league team selects a player. The order in which they choose is based on the team's standing in the previous season — the team that finished last chooses first, second to last chooses next, and so on. The major league rounds continue until all of the teams have made their selections. Then minor league teams make selections. Players who are selected earlier in the draft are obviously more in demand, and they can negotiate better terms.

"I was very naive. I was selected in the nineteenth round — just about the bottom third. My signing bonus was four thousand dollars, and I received only the minimum salary. I was immediately sent to the Billings Mustangs, Cincinnati's rookie league team in Montana, where I saw guys who were drafted before me but who didn't have any better physical tools than I did. It wasn't long before I led the team in hitting. I decided to concentrate completely on playing baseball. No books, no education, nothing on my mind except baseball. After the season, I had planned to go back to school. But baseball puts a lot of subtle pressures on its younger players. I was invited to an eight-week instructional league, a special league where the most promising players compete."

Reggie decided to stay with baseball. "The next two years, I played in Tampa, on the Class A League team. The first year, the first half of the season, I played very well. I was a guy who could hit singles and doubles. Because of my size — I'm over six feet tall — my manager told me to concentrate on home runs. My average went right down. Then after a season in another instructional league, I tore up my knee again and spent the winter in rehab. When I got back the following spring, I started swinging for power because the knee was not going to allow me to run fast

"I was immediately sent to the Billings Mustangs, where I saw guys who were drafted before me, but who were no better at hitting or fielding than I was. It wasn't long before I led the league in hitting."

enough to depend on singles and doubles. I started to change my swing to a power stroke in order to get the ball in the air — so I went away from the line drive stroke, started to strike out more, and I hit more home runs — but not enough! I had all of the tools that the scouts look for, but I had a difficult time putting things together.

"In my mind, I had fallen from prospect status to being just one of the guys. The next season, during spring training, I ended up on the lower Class A team in Shelby, North Carolina. By the end of my fourth year, I had not gone higher than Class A. But I had been around, and the younger guys started asking me questions. I found myself enjoying the teaching."

Not ready to give up the dream of playing, Reggie turned down a minor league coaching job within the Reds organization, and through the good work of a friend, he was traded to the Astros. With three days left in spring training, he started work with the Astros' A club in Daytona, Florida, hit over .300, and became a league leader. Meanwhile, his brother, Tye (Elliot Tyrone), was playing AA ball.

"For the second half of the season, I was promoted to Class AA in Columbus, Georgia — the Columbus Astros. My tools were good, but not as good as they used to be. I was getting older. I was already over twenty-four.

"Eventually, I ended up with a back problem and became a designated hitter. And I said to myself, Hey, Reggie, you're not staying healthy. It's time you started thinking about something else. It was the end of the dream for me, but I didn't want to just walk away. I figured I could go back to school — I could become a coach or maybe a manager. Someone suggested that I become a scout — but at the time, scouts were held in less esteem than used car salesmen. Then I realized that I could be a scout and go to school at the same time. Since the Astros didn't have a scout in the west, I decided to give scouting a try.

"When I became a scout, I started to see the game in a different light. I recalled the successful players who I had played with, the ones who made it to the major leagues, and I started using them as a benchmark. I concentrated on San Diego County to get an idea of what scouting was all about. Some scouts like to see Adonis bodies on their prospects, but that can be misleading. I remember Tony Gwynn — he had kind of a chubby body, his arm was below average, and he had thick ankles. I thought he was a good prospect, but it wasn't as simple as that. Two other scouts who worked with me — all three of us worked in combination for Texas, Seattle, and Houston — didn't believe in Tony's ability. One didn't think he was a prospect at all, and the other felt he was a marginal choice. I thought I had him pegged accurately, and I had information that Tony would be drafted by the NBA. One of the other guys thought I was crazy. The next day, Tony was drafted in the third round by the Padres and by the NBA. We lost out, but my confidence level was certainly increased by the incident with Tony. Some guys will fool you — Kirby Puckett, I remember, was the same type of player."

Scouting can be a humbling profession. If one in ten prospects makes it to the major leagues, that's considered good work. "You send some players out thinking they'll be great, but some get hurt, some don't have the work ethic, some have personality clashes with the development people and get buried. You need to learn as much about the player's personality as you can — it's not just the physical skills that make a major leaguer.

"The first guy I scouted who really got to the majors and stayed there was Donny August. I scouted him out of Chapman College in Southern California. He played on the U.S. Olympic baseball team and joined us in the Astros organization at instructional league. That first year, in Columbus, Georgia, he went 16 and 7, and everyone was on his bandwagon. Then he was traded to Milwaukee and played the end of the season with the Brewers. I was disappointed when he was traded; as a scout, you always hope that the people you select will make it all the way with your organization. But he's been up and down, in and out of the majors."

Of all the players that Reggie has scouted, Eric Anthony, a right fielder, is the one who is talked about most. "When I first saw Eric, it was not a pretty sight. They were throwing balls to him at first base, and he couldn't catch them. But he had a brutal arm and lots of power. The first time up, he hit a bolt right out of the ballpark. Next time up, he completely changed his approach; I questioned him about it, and he told me he was adjusting to the pitch he thought was on the way (when you hear something like that from a kid who never even played high school ball, it makes you wonder why he has that kind of instinct). Then, there were a few more bad fielding plays. But there was no doubt that he could hit."

Then Eric dropped out of sight. Reggie heard that Eric might be in some kind of trouble and tried to track him down. Reggie kept him on his list of possible candidates but started losing faith. "Then out of the blue, Eric called and provided me with all of the information I needed for the draft. He came to a practice and looked great, so we signed him. He went to a minor league team, but I heard he didn't play much. When I asked why, they told me that they had a lot of other outfielders. After the season, he just came home. So I started working with him."

Every day Reggie taught Eric the fundamentals. Eric was willing to work hard. The next year, he hit ten home runs with the Class A Gulf Coast League and was invited to instructional league. The following season, he moved up to the Class A South Atlantic League, where he hit twenty-nine home runs and his average topped .300. He worked his way up to play for the Houston Astros. He even hit a record-setting home run in the Astrodome (the record was for distance — the ball traveled about five hundred feet into the right field upper deck) and hit four home runs in four consecutive games. "Then Eric started to change. He was no longer willing to do the little things. He only wanted to hit the ball as far as he could. He was starting to make better money — and that can cause big changes in a kid from a disadvantaged background. Sometimes a young guy's shoulders aren't broad enough to handle the load of the big time."

Reggie was never happy with the training he received when he started scouting. So as he gained more experience, he volunteered to train any new personnel. Eventually he became the trainer for all new Astros scouts. He then became the western regional scouting supervisor in charge of Washington, Oregon, Arizona, Nevada, Idaho, Montana, Colorado, New Mexico, California, and Mexico.

"When you're working in the field as a scout, you travel a lot, but you don't make much money. You also don't get to set policy — you can only suggest young ballplayers who you would like to see in the organization. Since I wasn't making much money and was frustrated by the job, I decided to devote my full-time energies to the San Diego School of Baseball, which I had run for the past few years — the school was founded by Roger Craig, manager of the San Francisco Giants, former major leaguer Bob Skinner (best known as the hitting instructor for the Pittsburgh Pirates), and Bob Cluck (currently the pitching coach for the Houston Astros). Woody Woodward, a baseball executive with the Mariners, brought his son to my school. I think he liked the way I worked with the players and with the parents. We started talking every day. When I told Woody that I was going to leave the Astros to run the school full-time, he told me to reconsider. About two weeks later, Woody called to say that the game needed more young men like me. The following summer, he asked me to become his assistant.

"When I first became a scout, I wasn't sure whether I wanted to be an assistant general manager, a coach, or a scout. The Mariners gave me the opportunity to try some things, to see another part of baseball. Basically, I was involved in scouting players and evalu-

"When you're working in the field as a scout, you travel a lot, but you don't make much money."

Pony League:
An amateur baseball league similar to Little League.

Signing Bonus:
When a player signs a contract with a team, he may receive extra money up front. These bonuses range from a modest amount, such as a few thousand dollars, to much more, depending on how desirable the player is. A team may pay a high signing bonus to avoid paying higher yearly salaries later.

ating the Mariners organization. I had input on trades and did everything I could to help build the team.

"I knew Joe McIlvaine when he was director of scouting for the Mets; now he's the general manager of the Padres. When the new Colorado Rockies were putting together their staff, they hired Randy Smith as assistant general manager; he had been the director of scouting for the Padres. A number of people in the industry recommended me to Joe, and I was looking for the challenge of putting together a complete scouting operation and of implementing policy that would build the team over the long term. I was on a three-year contract with the Mariners, but the Padres called and asked for permission to speak with me about the scouting job. The Mariners were kind enough to allow me to talk to the Padres, which was their way of saying, 'If they offer you the job, you can go.'

"In my current position, I draw on all my years of experience. When you're young, you dream about the ways that you'd do the job if you had the chance. Now I've got the chance to provide direction to the scouts, to encourage them to find the best possible players for this organization. Specifically, I coordinate the efforts of the entire scouting team. I work with them to figure out how they should scout their areas. I teach them how to recognize the types of athletes we need in the Padres organization by looking for the physical tools I talked about earlier as well as a sound mental makeup. Each scout goes out to find the players and presents them in order of preference. We meet each year before the draft and decide on a draft order. Then we negotiate with the players in hopes that they will join our organization. I work very closely with the general manager, Joe McIlvaine, to find out what our needs are, and we try to address those needs through the draft."

Scouting for New Players

When Reggie was a scout, he made it known that he would grant a tryout to anyone who wanted one. Here's a rundown on what Reggie wants to see in a prospect.

"If you're a very good athlete, you've probably got a chance. To be a shortstop, you need fast hands, good arm strength, and good range. A second baseman can have a little less arm strength, but he must be able to turn a double play. A lot of guys who pitch in major league ball didn't pitch until they were fifteen or so. Many studies show that starting a pitcher too early — parents and coaches, take note — can be harmful. In a pitcher, I look for good mechanics, so the arm is not being harmed by the pitching action. Kids with classic arm action usually have no problem.

"If a player shows promise, the scout watches him during several games and workouts. An area scout assesses a player's physical attributes — his ability to run, throw, hit, hit with power, and field. He also looks at his overall size and strength. Prospects are graded on a scale of two to eight; two is the lowest score, and five is the average grade for a major league player. Based on major league standards, if you hit a ground ball, you should be able to consistently run to first base in 4.3 seconds if you're a right-handed hitter and 4.2 seconds if you're a left-handed hitter. If you can do this, you would be evaluated as a five. We look closely at mechanics. Does the prospect have a long swing or the short compact stroke that we prefer to see? Can he make consistent contact, especially when the game is on the line?

"Good athletes have a fluidity. They seem to glide. Average athletes don't flow to the ball. The exceptional athlete has a general awareness of the game — he seems to know what to do in every situation. He has good game sense. It doesn't seem to matter which sport the exceptional athlete is playing, you sense that keen awareness, those natural motions, and you know that you're seeing an exceptional kid. Scouts hear about the great ones before they ever see them. Marcus Allen played in the same Little League as my two younger brothers, and there was no doubt, even at age ten, that he was going to be a big star."

When a scout becomes interested in a particular candidate, he works up a chart that shows not only the player's current performance, but also his OFP, which is short for overall future potential. "If a guy is a five runner, for example, that's average for a major league runner. You try to rate the player based on what he is doing now and what he will probably be able to do in the majors. You try to estimate his future batting average, for example. This is difficult to do unless you see the player over a period of time. On any given day, the player may be especially good — or he may be having trouble. You're looking for something really special — scouting is so subjective — you're looking for a ball hit extra hard, but you're mainly looking for the basic tools, the fundamental skills that can be developed. You try to predict the player's future performance based on what you are seeing today."

Once a scout has completed the OFP, his work is cross-checked by another scout. If the other scout agrees, then the player's information is submitted to the director of scouting, who does some further cross-checking. If all goes well, both scouts meet the young athlete and arrange for a chat at home with the parents. A good scout will look out for both the interests of the team and the interests of the young player. If the player is interested in pro ball, then his name and other information is added to the team's draft list. The director of scouting and the team's general manager decide which players are most desirable and select one on each round of the major league draft. A total of 1,200 players or more are drafted by major league organizations each year.

Players negotiate for the best possible arrangement. Some are offered contracts while they're still in high school. Those who are confident of their abilities may be wise to go to college, play ball as often as possible, and sign after graduating. This is one way to avoid rookie league play, and it can improve a player's bargaining position. But it's not an easy decision — if a player turns down the contract at the time it's offered, the chance may never come again.

Reggie's ADVICE

"Until a few years ago, you had to be a ballplayer before you could be a scout. As the game has changed, that has changed as well. Now you must know the game of baseball, and you must know what to look for in a player.

"The best way to start is to learn what's expected of each player on the field. A shortstop should have speed and should be able to catch the ball. The first and third basemen should have power. Notice how guys apply themselves with the game on the line. If you have the ability to play, then play as long as you possibly can. You will learn more by playing than you will by watching. Go on to college and play, play, play. You may not be a major league prospect, but you will be learning all the time.

"Go to as many different games as you can. I don't mean just major league games. I mean major league, minor league, American Legion, college, high school, even Pony League. Be willing to learn, to listen. Learn how to approach scouts, and ask them how they judge players, what they look for, what their secrets are. The older scouts know the most — they've been around the longest. If you're serious about scouting, then offer to work for one of these scouts, for free, just to help out with paperwork. The training you get in return will be invaluable." There's a lot more to the job than just watching ball games — scouts collate information, do statistics, and spend lots of time evaluating, communicating, persuading, and negotiating.

"Not many people can say that they really enjoy what they do. My biggest thrill is to sit down with the parents and the kid and sign him up. I remember the thrill I felt when that happened to me." ■

General Manager
MIKE TATOIAN

Mike Tatoian is the general manager of the Quad City Angels, a minor league team.

Quad City is made up of Davenport and Bettendorf, Iowa, and Moline and Rock Island, Illinois.

Mike grew up in Bettendorf. John O'Donnell Stadium is located in Davenport.

B aseball has been a tradition in Quad City since the early 1900s. This stadium was built in 1931. It's a beautiful old stadium, right on the Mississippi River. My dad used to bring me here, but I never, ever thought that I'd end up working here."

When Mike was about eleven, he wanted to play baseball, and he became a solid third baseman. "Sports was everything to me. I was a die-hard Green Bay Packers fan, and the same for the St. Louis Cardinals and the Milwaukee Bucs. I was consumed with collecting baseball cards. My father was also a big, big sports fan. He worked as a laborer for a big aluminum company, but he was always taking me to games. We even went to the '67 and '68 World Series to see the Cardinals play. And as I started playing seriously, he was very much a part of what I was doing — he'd drive me everywhere and get really involved in the games."

In high school, Mike's main sports were football and wrestling. "I played football in the fall, usually offensive and defensive tackle, and I'd wrestle through the winter in the heavyweight division. I did track and field in the spring — discus and shot put — and in the summer, I played baseball. In my senior year, I was named athlete of the year. I hoped I'd either make it as a pro or as a coach or athletic director at a college. I got letters from a lot of Big Eight and Big Ten football schools, and I thought seriously about Brown, because they have a large Armenian student population, so I'd feel at home there. I also got a letter from Dan Gable, who won the gold medal for wrestling at the Olympics — he's from Waterloo, which is nearby — and he encouraged me to go into wrestling at the University of Northern Iowa. I went there on a football scholarship. I chose the school partly because I could play two sports there, while most other schools allowed only one in those days, and partly because the school's domed stadium eliminated any problems I'd have because of my asthma. It was also closer to home, and I wanted to be near my biggest fans — my parents, who had been such solid supporters. I also felt comfortable in a smaller school."

Mike knew he'd do fine academically regardless of his major, but he was drawn to a degree in physical education. "I knew all about what I call the jock syndrome — athletes who can't do much else so they become phys. ed. majors, but I felt I had something more to contribute. I had started to work with younger athletes in a parks and recreation department program during high school. I knew I wanted to work with kids. But I also knew that I could do something else if I wanted to."

College was more than just a place to play sports; it was a place where Mike learned a lot about himself. "In my junior year, I noticed for the first time how marketing and sports were interrelated. I saw, for example, that John Hancock sponsored the Sun Bowl and Sunkist sponsored the Orange Bowl, and I remember thinking, Hey, that's interesting how they put those pieces together. I took an advertising and marketing course to learn more about the field. And I started thinking about combining my athletic background with my interest in marketing. I became a pub-

lic relations major with a marketing minor, with the idea that I would do public relations work for a major league team."

Upon graduation, Mike returned home to Quad City but couldn't find the right job. "Plenty of people were knocking at my door, because I had played college sports and I was known locally. But I didn't want to use my reputation to sell insurance or copiers or office computer systems. I wrote letters to all of the teams in the Midwest, to Chicago, Minneapolis, St. Louis — but if I got any reply, it was usually a form letter saying that there were no openings at the present time. Realizing that Quad City was not the place to launch his career, Mike traveled to a larger city where he believed there would be greater opportunity: Tulsa, Oklahoma. "I had a friend down there who was doing well, and he told me I could stay at his place until I found something."

Mike's friend, who had grown up in Quad City, was a successful sales rep for a gutter company. Mike knew he didn't want to do that, but he did need a job within the next few months; after college, he had become engaged. A month later, Mike found a job at a health club, selling memberships and giving instruction. "It was a real nice health club, but I knew that working there was not going to further my career. Yet somehow or other, I knew I was going to succeed. I kept writing letters to major league teams, hoping to hear about an opening."

Mike got lucky. He noticed that several health club clients were especially athletic and that they wore baseball hats with the letter *T* on them. He worked up the nerve to ask them what the *T* stood for. "Tulsa Drillers," they answered. "We play AA ball in a Texas Rangers farm club."

Mike became friends with the players and eventually met the team's assistant general manager, who also worked out at the club. The assistant GM told Mike that he could come out to the ballpark whenever he wanted. The next night, Mike went out and asked for a job. Nothing was available at the time. "Even though there was no job, I started going to the ballpark all the time, partly to observe and partly because I wanted them to notice me. I should have taken a job selling popcorn, which would have gotten me involved with the organization, but the idea didn't occur to me until it was too late in the season. By October, I was calling them once a week. I had made the decision that I was going to bug them every week until they gave me a job!"

In the meantime, Mike enrolled at the University of Tulsa for a master's degree in sports management. He wasn't making enough money to pay for the courses, so he borrowed the money through the school's financial aid program.

Before Thanksgiving, Mike was also working part-time for the Tulsa Drillers. "They told me, 'Mike, we're going to try something we've never done before. It's called telemarketing. Your job will be to sell blocks of fifteen general admission tickets to organizations, for twenty-five dollars a block.' They offered me three-fifty per hour, plus a 10 percent commission on whatever I sold. I thought, If anyone finds out that I've got a college degree and I'm working for three-fifty an hour, they're going to think I'm crazy."

He did the job anyway.

"They let me set up a four-person office, with a three-month commitment. We worked from telephone books, just calling any organization that seemed promising. We sold more tickets than the team expected to. But the more important thing was that I got along great with the team. And when their groundskeeper left to take a job in another city, I asked for the job. Since I had never taken care of a baseball field before, I asked them to be very patient with me. The field was all turf, a really nice stadium. Well, they let me have the job."

Mike wasn't making much money — just a thousand dollars a month through the baseball season, with no promise of any work after the season, but his wife had a better job, and by combining their salaries, they were able to pay the rent. Mike continued to take classes at the University of Tulsa. "I was having the time of my life."

"When their groundskeeper left, I asked for the job. Since I had never taken care of a baseball field before, I asked them to be very patient with me."

At the end of the season, an administrative assistant job opened in the Drillers' front office. Mike jumped at the chance — and spent all of his time selling ads for the Drillers' program. The best thing about the job was that it was a permanent position; Mike's salary was guaranteed unless he was either fired or left on his own. "Unlike most minor league teams, the Drillers were owned by the major league team, so my paycheck actually said Texas Rangers on it. My checks were drawn on the same account as the checks paid to the players! I know that may seem like a little thing, but it was a big thrill for me at the time."

The Tulsa Drillers became a larger organization, and Mike moved up, eventually to become the director of media relations. He spent three seasons with Tulsa, learned a great deal about minor league ball, and discovered that baseball management was a career that he wanted to pursue. In Tulsa's general manager, Joe Preseren, Mike had an excellent role model and mentor. "Joe told me that I was capable of doing the general manager job, that I was well suited to that kind of work."

Most of the general managers and owners in the Texas League knew that Mike was looking for his first GM job. It was only a matter of time before an opportunity would open up. When Mike Feder, the GM of the Jackson (Mississippi) Mets, left for another position, Mike Tatoian contacted Jackson owner Richard Holtzman, whom he knew. But things did not go as Mike had planned.

"Richard didn't give me the job in Jackson. Instead, he told me that Mike Feder had gone to work with a new A-league team that Richard had just bought. Richard's plan was to have me work there as assistant GM for a year, and then to move Mike Feder to a new AAA team in Arizona and make me the new general manager of the A-league team. I accepted the assistant GM slot with the new team."

There are baseball teams located all over the country. This

particular baseball team was located in a place Mike never thought he would see again: Quad City, Iowa.

"The stadium was in terrible shape. It was a pit. But when I learned that the city was going to spend over three million dollars to fix up the old place, and I heard Richard's plans for the team and for me, I accepted the job. Besides, there was something special about coming home."

In just one year, the new management more than doubled stadium attendance, from 44,000 to 115,000. Just as planned, the stadium was renovated. At the end of the season, Mike Feder left for the Tucson Toros, an AAA team, and Mike Tatoian was prepared to take over the Quad City Angels. Then he was offered the assistant GM job in Tucson. "I called Joe Preseren, my friend and former boss in Tulsa, and asked for advice. He told me to stay in Iowa, and that's exactly what I did. He was right — I needed to do the job on my own. So I started putting pressure on myself to get fans into the ballpark, to dig down and really market the team locally. In my first year as GM, we drew 192,000 people. I think the stadium renovation helped; we created a nice family atmosphere, a good place to be during the summer. We used to draw a big drinking crowd — loud, boisterous, sometimes even a little dangerous. Now we draw families, even mothers with babies. It's quite a change."

Mike has become one of the leading promoters in his league. When his Angels hosted the Midwest League All-Star game, they threw a party that the league will not soon forget. "From eleven until two, we hosted a three-hour riverboat ride down the Mississippi for everyone in the league. It was open to the public, so they could have lunch with the players, collect autographs, and have a great time. Dan Quisenberry, the Kansas City great, was the guest speaker. We gave special All-Star watches to each of the players. At four, when the players took batting practice, the stadium was open to fans. AT&T Long Distance sponsored a

"We used to draw a big drinking crowd — loud, boisterous, sometimes even a little dangerous. Now we draw families to the stadium, even mothers with babies."

home run contest. Dan Quisenberry took some swings. Mainly, it was a contest between league all-stars; the winners received cordless phones. For every home run, we contributed twenty-five dollars to a local charity. Throughout the afternoon and into the evening, we gave out goodies to the fans: miniature bats, special key chains. We hired a Dixieland band to play before the game and between innings. Hot air balloons — including one shaped like a baseball and another one that looked like a huge pig — were launched from the outfield. As soon as the balloons were up, five sky divers with smoke grenades jumped down from the balloons, and landed on the bases and the pitcher's mound. That's when the national anthem was played. Then during the game, we gave away Caribbean cruises and trips to see the St. Louis Cardinals and the Chicago Cubs. After the game, we had a huge fireworks display over the Mississippi. And, finally, the front office people threw a big barbeque for the players and their families. I figured that we had a chance to show off what our organization could do, to take our place in the league. I prayed that everything would work as planned. It was a big event for us."

Mike supervises a small staff of full-time employees. Kerry Bubolz is the assistant general manager. David Fisher is the team's broadcaster; he does play-by-play on 140 games every year for KSTT, and he writes game notes for other reporters. Lesley Kellison is the director of group ticket sales. Bill Marcus is director of concessions; he's in charge of food and souvenir sales. Chris Holvoet is the team's administrative assistant, and Pam Verre is the team's secretary. In addition, between fifty and seventy-five part-timers work at the games, mostly at the concessions.

"At this level, pulling tarps on rainy days is my job, too. If you know that there's a problem in a rest room, and you're the one who's nearby, you'd better take care of it. I don't care what anyone's job title is — we all pitch in. We try to do everything right, even though we're in a place that many people might

Part of Mike's job is to sell advertising space on the Angels' outfield signs.

consider to be small-time. We used to sell advertising space on our outfield signs for $500 to one company for the season, maybe $1,000 to another one. Now we charge $1,950 for each sign, and because of the increased attendance, we have a waiting list. Since we've really done all of this in just two years — it used to be me, the general manager, and the GM's wife doing everything — I'm really proud of what we've been able to do here."

Mike will probably move on to another GM job in a larger city, most likely with an AA and then an AAA team. Alternately, he'd like to join a major league team, or perhaps an NFL or NBA team, in public relations or in sports marketing. Someday, he'd like to get back to working directly with the players, most likely in a player development position.

"But when I close my eyes and try to visualize my life ten years down the road, here's what I see: I see myself as part of a major sports marketing organization, an important person at the company who's negotiating a deal with a major national insurance company to sponsor the Rose Bowl or the All-Star game. I like that dream even more than I do the one about owning and managing my own minor league team."

Lingo

Sports Marketing:
A special type of marketing that combines advertising with sporting events. Examples include Panasonic's sponsorship of racing cars; Chrysler's large cash awards in the Kentucky Derby, the Preakness Stakes, and the Belmont Stakes; and the tote bags given away by soft drink companies at baseball parks every year.

Mike's ADVICE

"In this job, you really don't have to know the intricacies of the game of baseball. Knowing that the pitcher is going to throw a curveball isn't going to help me to fill the stands."

Mike's advice for students is simple and straightforward. "Do what you're supposed to do in school. Get a good solid education. Stay active, and get involved in extracurricular activities. If you're near a ballpark, or any college or professional sports facility, get a job as a vendor, selling hot dogs or popcorn or drinks or whatever. You'll develop a sense of how long the hours are and how an organization operates. Stay in school, and don't feel that you must know exactly what you want to do when you get out. I didn't know what I wanted to do until I was out of college."

As preparation for a general manager job, Mike recommends a major in marketing, communications, or business, probably with some course work in accounting. He also recommends starting "low on the totem pole" and working your way up.

"Go to the annual winter meetings. They hold seminars for college graduates who want to get jobs. You'll see a few hundred students there. Most of them are competing for jobs that pay less than $1,000 a month. Nobody comes into minor league ball at $30,000."

Once you get started, you will almost certainly have some tasks that you don't want to do. "If you're in charge of the bathrooms, make sure that your bathrooms are the cleanest in the league. People will notice." ∎

Stadium Operations Executive
TERRY SAVARISE

Building a major league baseball stadium can be an overwhelming task. We're installing 725 telephones, a restaurant that overlooks the field and seats over 300 people, a sports bar for over 400, offices, rest rooms, tens of thousands of seats, a hall of fame, food stands, press and media facilities — the list goes on and on. If I try to step back and look at the whole job, it's overwhelming, so I take things one step at a time and focus on the details."

Growing up in Ashtabula, Ohio, Terry was a fan of the Cleveland Indians and the Cleveland Browns. He collected baseball cards, went to Little League games, sat on his back porch and listened to baseball coverage on the radio, and tried to convince his parents to take him to the stadium. "I spent a lot of time thinking about sports, but no more than any other kid my age. I was a pretty good center fielder and later a good infielder, and even though I had the dream of playing in the big leagues, I knew I didn't have the talent. When I was a senior in high school, I decided I wanted to work for a professional baseball team. I read an article in our local newspaper about the man who did public relations for the Indians. I called him at work, and he agreed to meet me. My father and

Terry Savarise is the vice president in charge of stadium operations for the Chicago White Sox.

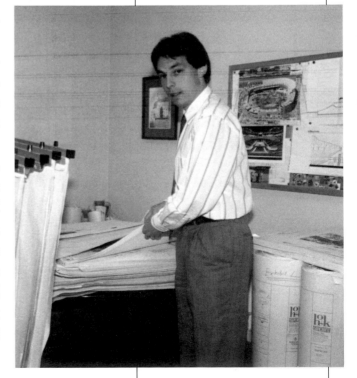

69

I drove up to Cleveland. Nothing really happened at the meeting, but I learned a little about the way that the baseball business works. And I got some encouragement."

Terry attended Ohio University, where he concentrated on business courses. As an undergraduate, looking for a taste of life in the front office of a professional team, Terry arranged an internship with the Cleveland Cavaliers in the NBA. "I was free labor for them. I sold tickets and did some accounting work. But I learned a lot just by being there.

"When I wasn't studying or going to classes, I was involved with extracurricular activities, like counseling support groups or tutoring athletes. I was also the assistant to the baseball coach. I mainly concentrated on raising money to pay for the team's travel. Going to the state American Legion tournament was a big deal, and I helped raise money for that."

Ohio University's master's program in sports administration is highly regarded; Terry was accepted in the program, worked hard, and finished in just one year with a 3.8 grade point average. "One of the benefits of enrollment in OU's program is visibility. Teams send people to the school to interview students who are about to graduate. Since I had a good mix of course work (a few public relations courses and broadcasting courses outside the major, which I took because media is such a big force in professional sports), good grades, an internship with a professional team, and a lot of extracurricular work, I was a good candidate. I had a few offers, mainly from professional football teams — I could have had four Super Bowl rings by now, but I have no regrets. I really wanted to work in baseball." Eventually, he found a job with the Chicago White Sox in the accounting department.

"It started as a three-month paid part-time internship, but it turned into a full-time job. I worked with the controller on a new budgeting system, new procedures for the purchasing department, that sort of thing. I was helping a new management team —

who had bought the White Sox from Bill Veeck — organize a more efficient business operation. I spent a lot of time writing checks, bookkeeping, and organizing and making entries in the general ledger. If you want to know how a team's business works, there is no better place to be than the accounting office. You see everything — you see the guts of the organization."

Terry was proving himself, showing that he was capable of taking on more responsibility. "I started working on player contracts and on a financing package for our new SuperSuites. Then I got involved with a tax-exempt bond issue and with escrow accounts with banks." Within two years, he was named assistant to the controller, and two years later, he became controller and then vice president of stadium operations.

While Terry was still the assistant controller, the White Sox's chairman asked him if he'd like to get involved in something new. "He told me that we'd eventually have to leave Comiskey Park and asked me if I'd like to evaluate possible relocation sites."

Terry spent the better part of that first year on a fact-finding mission. He visited baseball stadiums, football stadiums and arenas — facilities of every shape and size. He talked with architects, learning who built stadiums and why some were better than others. He spent a lot of time in Toronto, where the new Skydome was being built for the Blue Jays. "I learned about how strong soil would have to be in order to support a stadium, about community reactions to a baseball stadium in the neighborhood, and about the Environmental Protection Agency and its rules."

Two years into the process, Terry was asked to supervise the design and construction of the new White Sox training complex in Sarasota, Florida. "I looked at all of the big league training sites and used the best ideas to create something that would meet our needs. The politicians were all very supportive, and so was the community. It was a good testing ground for me, a good way to learn what I was doing while working on a smaller scale."

Meanwhile, he continued to research possible sites for a new

"If you want to know how a team's business works, there is no better place to be than the accounting office."

White Sox park. Promoters and politicians from cities all over the country tried to persuade the team to move; St. Petersburg, Florida looked promising for a long while. Still, Terry, the team's management, and the fans wanted the White Sox to stay in Chicago. In time, he identified twenty sites in the Chicago area where a new stadium might be built, some in downtown Chicago, others in the suburbs. "The suburban sites were a problem from the beginning, because there weren't enough politicians from any one area to give us the support in local and state government that we needed. Eventually we found a site that we liked and politicians from the city sponsored a financing bill in the state government, but it didn't pass. We tried for another suburban site, but that didn't work out either.

"Then the city came back to us and said that they had a site, one that was already accessible by major highways. After a very hectic week of lobbying senators and representatives, the state decided that the White Sox were very important to Chicago and to Illinois. The state created the Sports Authority, granted the land, and gave us the money to build the stadium. We broke ground five years after my first memo. I knew that the work would be hard and that the hours would be long, but I never expected the job to be so consuming, so complicated, and, to be honest, so much fun.

"I started by writing a forty-page outline of what I thought the new stadium would need. For example, I knew that the clubhouse area would need a manager's office, a larger locker room area, a training room, a laundry room, and so on, and I knew that some of these

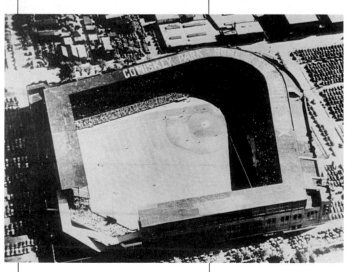

Two views of the old Comiskey Park. The new stadium was built directly across the street.

places had special size, electrical, and plumbing requirements. I worked with the HOK Sports Facilities Group, an architectural firm that specializes in sports complexes and convention centers. So I knew what the team needed, and the HOK people not only knew how to design and build a stadium but also what other teams had done. I figured, 'I don't know how to do this, so the next best thing is to hire someone who's really an expert.' I made the right decision."

Based on the written outline and their own surveys of the site, the architectural firm prepared a series of drawings to plan the project further. They began with general drawings, called schematics, that showed the overall structure, the larger pieces to be constructed, and the way in which the building was going to be positioned on the site. These drawings were useful in planning traffic patterns, parking, the direction of the sun (if the stadium is positioned incorrectly, the sun will prevent the batters or outfielders from being able to see the ball).

A second set of planning documents was drawn up, consisting of more detailed drawings that showed the design of individual facilities. In the bathrooms, for example, where would the sinks be? How large would they be? How many? Would there be a changing area for infants? How many parents could be in that area at a time? Thousands of questions were raised and ultimately answered in meetings and phone conversations. Every stadium is different; every team and every facility has its own special needs. Drawings were made for the restaurants, the hallways (Where would the access ramps begin and end? Where would the telephones be? How many telephones?), the clubhouse, the media

"I knew that the work would be hard and that the hours would be long, but I never expected the job to be so consuming, so complicated, and, to be honest, so much fun."

An architect's model of the new Comiskey Park, created before construction began.

Lingo

Controller:
A company's senior executive in charge of accounting.

SuperSuites:
Small enclosed living rooms with balconies whose seats overlook the playing field. SuperSuites are usually rented, at high prices, to area corporations for use by executives and company clients.

Tax-Exempt Bond:
A means of raising large sums of money. A bond is a kind of loan that pays interest to anyone. Because it's tax exempt, taxes do not have to be paid on the interest. Tax-exempt bonds are often used to raise money for major civic construction projects.

Escrow Account:
Monies safely deposited in a lawyer's account that cannot be withdrawn until the terms of a contract are fulfilled.

Environmental Protection Agency (EPA):
The U.S. government agency charged with protecting the natural environment. The EPA usually has to approve large construction projects.

area, the ticket takers' room, and the umpires' room. Everything had to be planned in advance, so that parts and equipment could be ordered, designed, modified, and delivered in time for installation.

The third set of drawings was the construction blueprints. For the new Comiskey Park, the book of blueprints is three thousand pages long. The White Sox and the Illinois Sports Facilities Authority, the state government agency responsible for selling the bonds and hiring the contractor, pre-approved several contractors for each job, based largely on whether they had experience building similar facilities. Each contractor prepared a bid, and each job went to the lowest bidder. Individual contractors were responsible for concrete, glass, electrical lines, telephone lines, plumbing — a very long list. On any given day, more than five hundred people were at work on the project, sometimes as many as a thousand.

The first step in the construction process was demolition. "That was probably the hardest part," Terry explains. "There were a few successful businesses on that site, stores that had been operating for decades. They were destroyed to make way for the new building."

Shortly after demolition, the contractor laid the foundation — 510 big round footings, each sunk eighty feet into the ground. Then the building started to take shape. The biggest part of the job was pouring concrete to create the physical structure. In order to retain the old-fashioned flavor of the original park, precast concrete was manufactured, using Comiskey's original design, and hung up piece by piece around the exterior of the stadium. "It's rose colored. That was the original color of the old park, before it was whitewashed. We tried to retain as much of the old place as we could. We're replicating the original scoreboard, but the new one will be more modern in its operation. We even trucked in the infield dirt from the old stadium. The players like the original dirt — they asked for it."

As the construction moved ahead, Terry started working with the concessions company to determine what would be sold at the stadium. "We wanted to offer the same variety as we had in the old park. We kept Eddie, the shoe shine guy. We kept the same basic foods, but we came up with some new names and new designs for the food stands. We added two big novelty stores and a nice hall of fame."

Even color became an issue. "The old stadium had green seats, which were great because they gave the feeling of a nice old park. But we did blue seats in Sarasota, and they look so good that we're going with blue seats in the new park. We'll still have about three thousand bleacher seats in the outfield, though, because the fans seem to like them."

With the new Comiskey Park completed for the 1991 season, Terry is concerned with making everything work as he planned. The park is beautiful — fans seem to enjoy the facility, and the media has been quite positive as well. He's also paying attention to new challenges. One of the youngest executives in baseball, Terry could move up within the White Sox organization. With his understanding of the business side of the game, he might someday take charge of a team's operations. He might also move to another team and take charge of another major project. Optimistic about the future, he has already started planning the next project: a 22,000-seat state-of-the-art arena for the Bulls (NBA) and the Blackhawks (NHL).

Schematics:
Detailed drawings that show how a building is to be constructed.

Blueprints:
Photographic reproductions of construction plans in white on a blue background.

Contractor:
A person or company that contracts with a buyer to provide construction or other services.

Footings:
Cement blocks, buried deep in the ground, that support a large structure such as a building.

Terry at the construction site for the new park.

Terry's ADVICE

"I was fortunate, but I was also flexible. I was presented with a good opportunity, and I agreed to try something new."

When Terry was working in the accounting department and was asked to research baseball stadiums, he never dreamed that he would become the man in charge of building the White Sox's new home. "I tried to project ahead, to see myself learning more and more about stadiums, and eventually taking charge. It was a dream then, but I remember long conversations with my father; we both knew I could do this job.

"When you're twelve or thirteen or fourteen years old, I know it's hard to prepare for a career. There's so much that you don't know about the way things work, but if a subject interests you, then you've got to get out there and learn all you can. The most important thing is to stay in school. Read books, newspapers, magazines — anything you can get your hands on. Then start calling people who work in the industry; ask permission to watch them at work, to ask questions, to help out in the office. If you contact the minor league clubs, you'll find that they'll be happy to hear from you, that they want and need the help, and that you'll get as much responsibility as you can handle. You'll sell at the concessions, you'll pull the tarp when it rains, you'll run errands, you'll sell tickets, and you'll learn what goes into making a baseball team work."

When you start thinking about college, remember that baseball is a business. "We need good solid businesspeople. When I see a resume, I want to see a substantial background in the sports business or a related profession. We're very much a 'people business,' so experience putting people together to accomplish goals is very important. Don't stop at sports management courses, though. Take classes in areas that will help you in the sports business. Take courses in television, for example, and learn what the difference is between a rating and a share, or in public relations, where you can learn to write a press release or prepare an information kit."

Finding a first job is a major challenge. "It takes perseverance. It's easier, of course, if you've done an internship. Try calling on alumni from your college — they may help you along. If you don't have the contacts, then write lots and lots of letters, attend the winter meetings, and get out to meet people. Start in the minors — they don't just train the players; they train a lot of front office people as well." ■

Stadium Entertainer
NANCY FAUST

T wo eleven-year-old girls peer through a dirty Plexiglas window, pointing and giggling. They point at Nancy and her keyboards. They giggle because Nancy Faust has agreed to play their request, a Paula Abdul song, "Straight Up."

Nancy and her keyboards are located in seating section number 132, in the lower deck, directly behind home plate. She works in a booth that's accessible to fans, so she can have fun with them. She is, as much as any player or the team's manager, a star of the Chicago White Sox.

"I know that I can be replaced by a tape cartridge machine. So I try to keep things fresh and original. I think live music makes a big difference. I'm spontaneous — I invent things that a tape cartridge couldn't possibly do. But mainly, I listen to the fans. I get most of my ideas from them."

The pre-game conversation is interrupted by a fan. "It's my wife's birthday. Can you play 'Happy Birthday' to her?" Nancy's answer is a simple "Yes." She plays the song every night; it's always somebody's birthday.

"I started out like any other kid. My parents had to encourage me to practice. I loved horses, and if I practiced, my dad would take me out horseback riding. That was good incentive."

Nancy Faust plays the organ during Chicago White Sox games at Comiskey Park.

"Nancy, we miss you at the Hawks games," says another fan. "You gotta get back to hockey. We're gonna write them a letter to get you back in." Nancy smiles and replies, "All they have to do is hire me.

"I came from a musical family," she continues. "My mom played, and she gave me a lot of encouragement. Here in Chicago, there used to be a television show called *Morris B. Sacks' Amateur Hour*. I was on, and I played the song 'Glow Worm.' I kept improving — I guess I was pretty good for my age. I've seen kids who were child prodigies. That wasn't me. I was just someone who could play, who practiced so I got better and better. When I was ten, I was on a national show, *Arthur Godfrey's Talent Scouts*."

"Excuse me, Nancy. Can you play the New Kids on the Block song 'The Right Stuff'? You can? Wow! Really? Nancy, you're great!"

"I try to be real accessible to fans. And I try to keep up with the latest songs, but it doesn't come without a lot of practice time. Anyway, when I was about eleven or twelve, I got a job on weekends, playing a Hammond organ in a store. The idea was that the organ was so easy to use, even a child could do it. The man who actually demonstrated the organ was Shay Torrent, who played here at the stadium for seven years. Hang on. . . ."

The game is getting started. Nancy, wearing headphones, hears her first cue from the scoreboard room. She plays the theme from *The Muppet Show* ("Why don't we get things started . . .") and then a sixties rock tune called "Something Tells Me I'm into Something Good." When the stadium P.A. announcer shouts, "Ladies and gentlemen, here are your Chi-ca-go White Sox," Nancy plays "Chicago (That Toddlin' Town)," and the White Sox take the field. Nancy plays a fanfare, and more than 25,000 people cheer.

"I was more interested in pets than sports. When I was twelve, I had a white rat. We lived in the northwestern part of the city. Hang on."

The first opposing player is out. She plays "So Long, It's Been Good to Know Yuh."

Nancy points to a fan seated nearby. "That guy in the blue shirt, he knows my whole routine. When I play something new, he turns around and lets me know his opinion. These people are *serious* White Sox fans; they come to a lot of games. There are a lot of regulars here. Every winter, we have a box 132 party, and a lot of the people come."

The inning is over. Just before the White Sox come up, Nancy plays "I'm a Believer," an old Monkees song.

"I really had no idea that this would be my career. In high school, I just hung out with my friends. I was a good student, but nothing special, maybe in the top third of my class. I played the flute in the band for three years. And when it was time for college, I just picked a school nearby. I waited until my third year to select a major; I figured I would teach elementary school, so I became an education major with a psychology minor."

Many of her college friends were male. There was a lot of talk about sports in general and baseball in particular. A few friends encouraged Nancy to promote her musical talents — to write letters to the Chicago Bears, Bulls, Blackhawks, Cubs, and White Sox. "I enclosed one of my brochures — I had been picking up extra money playing the organ at conventions and parties. Apparently, the White Sox kept my letter on file, and when the club had a falling out with their organ player, they called me! They told me to just show up one day and play. Fortunately, it was one of the worst seasons in history, so I picked a good year to . . . Hang on."

First, a fast fanfare. Nancy seems to be able to carry on a conversation while watching the game. She rarely misses an opportunity for a musical cue. There's a man on base. She plays "If You're Happy and You Know It, Clap Your Hands," and thousands of hands clap on her cue. The inning ends.

It's time for The Great CTA Bus Race.

On the scoreboard, three CTA (Chicago Transit Authority) buses race around a track. Nancy plays the William Tell Overture (the *Lone Ranger* theme). The red bus wins in a photo finish.

"I remember that first day: I was pretty scared. I got a rundown of which state each player was from, and I tried to match songs to state names, like 'California, Here I Come.' If the guy's name was John, I played the theme from *The Tonight Show,* making the connection to Johnny Carson. I had the right idea, but it took me a long time to develop my repertoire."

Nancy works with a large Technics electronic organ with a full pedal board, plus an Ensoniq SQ80 electronic keyboard, a sequencer, and a drum machine. She has encoded rhythm patterns and keeps the list on a sheet of cardboard wrapped in plastic to protect it from the weather.

"When Bill Veeck owned the team, the place was like a giant saloon, lots of colorful characters, a very rowdy crowd. That was a good time. Now the new owners have cleaned up the act, and we get a lot of families. I never get tired of it. I like to be around the fans. When I get an idea, I just try it out, and if it works, I use it again."

"Hey, Nancy, can I have your autograph?" Nancy keeps a pile of baseball cards on her organ. She signs one. She's probably one of the only women in baseball whose face is featured on a baseball card. "The team prints them," she explains. "They're not available from any of the card companies."

She interrupts the conversation with a pumping rhythm track. It's starting to look like the White Sox are going to win the game. There's a man on base. Carlos Martinez hits a line drive to the outfield and scores the winning run. Nancy plays "Hallelujah!" and then "Na Na Hey Hey Good-bye." The scoreboard goes crazy with streaming pinwheels and chasing lights. She plays along. Then as the crowd disperses, she packs up, signs a few more baseball cards, shuts down her equipment, and heads for home.

Nancy's ADVICE

"I'm concerned about the future. It's not that the parks don't want live music. The problem is there aren't many people learning to play the organ these days. I heard that the Orioles want an organist, but they're having trouble finding one. It will have to be someone who can think fast, who has a good repertoire and a good ear. I know that some teams have eliminated their organ players — that happened at Shea Stadium, in New York, and Busch, in St. Louis — and it's always a threat, especially if your music doesn't change with the times. But I think the organ is an important part of a stadium's entertainment. The fans have to respond, though, and the organ player has to bring something that recorded music cannot. It's a delicate balance."

Nancy believes that half of all major league parks would employ organ players if there were enough good players to go around. She also points out that "things go in cycles. One year, the organ player might be replaced by recorded music. Then new management takes over, or the old management wants to return to a tradition, and all of a sudden, there's an opportunity."

To get started, practice every day. "You'll need a musical education, a good ear, and as large a repertoire as possible. You need to be aware of popular songs and their titles, and you have to do your own arrangements. I think it's best if this is something that you really want to do. Once you feel that you have it down, get in touch with area ballparks and let them know that you're out there. Write to the general manager and the marketing director. And don't forget the minor leagues — there are more teams in the minors than there are in the majors, and it's usually easier to get in."

In addition to baseball, Nancy suggests contacting basketball and hockey teams. But, she adds, "baseball lends itself best to live music." ■

Baseball Operations Managers
KEN and STEVE LEHNER

Ken Lehner is the baseball operations manager for the Buffalo Bisons, a minor league team. His younger brother, Steve, is the assistant baseball operations manager.

Our ultimate goal is to see a local boy from Buffalo playing major league baseball in his hometown. We see this as a long-term commitment. We're establishing an identity in this community; we do a lot of teaching, working with kids in the city and in the area. We run a lot of baseball clinics every year, here at Pilot Field, at schools, and in playgrounds. We're deeply committed to youth baseball; we run a rookie league, where just being part of the team is more important than winning. We run a Pitch, Hit & Run championship every year. Why do we do all of this? Because it's good business. We're training players while they're young; we're becoming an important part of the Buffalo community by concentrating on youth; and we hope that these people will become lifelong Bisons fans."

The Buffalo Bisons are a relatively new AAA franchise, the top farm team for the Pittsburgh Pirates. They're an ambitious team with a new stadium, Pilot Field, which was built in a renovated downtown section of town and designed to be easily converted into a major league stadium. It's a park with an old-fashioned feel, within walking distance of Buffalo's office buildings and shopping centers. During the season, the park is open during the day for lunch; local fans can drop by and eat or relax. "It's just another way of saying, Hey, we're here, we want to be a part of life in Buffalo."

Ken and Steve were born and raised in Buffalo, less than three miles from Pilot Field. Ken was "addicted to baseball." He played in grammar school, in the Police Athletic League, in Little League, and in the American Legion League. He was also co-captain of his high school championship team. At one point, he was playing for three different teams, riding his bicycle as much as ten miles a day to the games. When he wasn't playing organized ball, Ken played Wiffle ball or stickball in the backyard.

During the winter, Ken played ice hockey. A man named Bob Rich, Jr., coached the team. "Bob was a great coach. I remember one year, when I didn't make the older boys' team, I was really upset. He reassured me, told me that I'd eventually become the team's star center. When the season was over, he gave all of us trophies and told us we had had a great season. Then he said something special to me, something that I'll always remember. He said, 'Ken, I'd like to have you on my team forever.' I didn't know what he meant, but it sure sounded great."

A few years later, when the Bisons were doing so poorly that the franchise was ready to fold, Bob Rich, Jr., bought the team and became a local hero. Ken wrote him a letter to thank him for saving the team. In it he described how much he and his family enjoyed going to the Bisons games at the old Buffalo War Memorial and boldly offered that if there was *anything* he could do to help the team (be a bat boy, for instance), to please call.

A week later, Mike Billoni, the Bisons' general manager, showed up at the Lehners' door. "He brought boxes of newspa-

per articles about the Bisons that had been published over the past hundred years. He asked me to put together a scrapbook. That was the beginning of my life with the Bisons."

That summer, Ken spent most of his time at War Memorial. "I'd go to the games for free and just help out. That was the summer I got my Dave Gallagher bat. I still have it sitting next to my bed." Ken worked with the team, without getting paid, through the following winter. "I wrote most of the Christmas cards that year, stuffed envelopes, learned how to do season ticket sales and actually sold a few to neighbors; I even sold some ads for the program."

The next summer, when he was sixteen, Ken worked in the press box, operating the scoreboard, and for the public relations department, preparing game notes, answering phones, and keeping statistics. When the Bisons started a baseball operations department, Ken began working with the Indians and the Pirates organizations and with their respective managers, coaches, and players. (The Indians and the Pirates jointly used Buffalo as a farm team in those days.)

When he was ready for college, Ken did not want to stop working with the team, and the team was reluctant to lose him. "I went to Fordham, in New York City. The team would fly me home to work on weekends during April and May. I don't know of any other team that's so concerned about its employees."

Since Fordham University is not far from Yankee Stadium, Ken was able to work for the Yankees during one school year. "They offered me a position, and I worked there part-time for six months. The Bisons refused to hire anyone to replace me; they held my job open until I decided whether I'd stay with the Yan-

Ken Lehner at his desk. The board behind him lists all of the players in the Pirates' major and minor league operations.

84

kees. I decided to return to the Bisons — a choice I've never regretted."

Steve followed his brother into the Bisons organization. "My parents threw a party for Ken when he graduated from high school. They invited a lot of Bisons employees. And I remember that Mike Billoni, the GM, stopped me just before he left to say, 'So, Steve, when are you going to start working with us?' I took him seriously, and the very next game, I went over to the stadium. I went right to work, bringing messages to members of the press, getting food for the media, taking information from the sports ticker to the reporters and our stadium P.A. announcer. A short time later, I took over the scoreboard. At the end of that first year, I wrote all of the team's Christmas cards. I did that every day after school for weeks. While Ken was away at Fordham, I remained involved with the team. At the same time, I kept up with sports on my own. Like Ken, I had always played baseball, and also hockey."

Today, together with one secretary and some interns, Steve and Ken are the baseball operations department for the Bisons. Ken explains, "We are the connection between the Bisons and the Pirates. We run the day-to-day AAA minor league operation according to the terms of the player development contract, the standard agreement between major and minor league teams." Under that agreement, the Pirates supply twenty-three players for the roster. The Pirates also provide a manager, but the choice is discussed with the Bisons. The major league team gives a lump sum to the minor league team for player salaries, bonuses, meal money, and some expenses. "This can get complicated, because we receive large reimbursement checks from the Pirates, and we must break them down ourselves before paying the bills. Our job is a little like the traveling secretary at the major league level — we take care of travel and hotel arrangements. We also provide the equipment and uniforms. We file daily injury reports and send copies to the manager of the Bisons, our trainer, the Pittsburgh front office, and the team doctor."

Ken was able to work for the Yankees during one school year. "Meanwhile, the Bisons refused to hire anyone else to replace me. I decided to return to the Bisons — a choice I've never regretted."

Steve Lehner at the controls for the Bisons' scoreboard.

Steve is very strong in computer applications. "We are constantly setting up new ways of keeping records on the computer system," Ken explains. "Steve is in charge of all of that."

Both Ken and Steve work directly with the players in several different ways. First, they take care of the players' personal needs. "When a new player comes to town, we help him find an apartment. In addition, we arrange for rental cars, furniture, and installation of utilities." On a single night, Steve cashed fourteen thousand dollars in players' personal checks, just for spending money. When an expense check comes in from Pittsburgh, Steve breaks it down. "The players get eighteen dollars a day in meal money, but if the team is away for ten and a half days, then it gets a little more complicated. And if you owe major league meal money to some players but not to others, the whole thing becomes a little *more* complicated. Doing those expenses really puts your ninth grade algebra skills to the test."

"You never know what's going to happen," Ken points out. "Just when we're in the middle of a clinic, a rookie league session, or a staff meeting, we might get a call that a new player is coming into the airport. One of us gets into the car, usually fighting traffic, to get the new player and bring him back to the stadium in time for that night's game."

During the game, Steve operates the scoreboard, eats his dinner, and watches the action. Ken stops by several times, but he's usually busy with VIPs or problem solving. He often watches the game with the scouts that are in the stadium. "I'm also around for injuries. I remember one game, a player broke his elbow. I took him to the hospital and stayed with him. As soon as I got back, someone else got hit with a line drive and broke his nose, so it was back to the hospital. Taking care of players — both the Bisons and the visiting team — is part of what I'm paid to do."

After the game, Ken and Steve spend about an hour taking care of player requests such as hotel reservations for family and friends and ticket requests for upcoming games. They also set up player interviews with the media and confirm player appearances for the next day. Finally, they fax the game report to the director of minor league operations in Pittsburgh.

Although Ken and Steve are about the same age as the players and much of their time is spent working with them, the Lehners are clearly part of the team's management. "You can't really become too friendly with the players. If you get emotionally involved, it's going to be a problem. Also, the players don't stay around — they move from one team to another. That's tough if you're becoming friends."

Still in his early twenties, Ken is a serious baseball executive. "I get locked into a lot of meetings. I am the Bisons' representative in our dealings with equipment companies, hotels, airlines, Little Leagues, and other vendors. There are big blocks of time when I have to be in specific places. When someone is needed to talk about baseball, I go. I also go with the players to community events and clinics. After the players finish the clinic, I stay with the people in the community and talk about arrangements for next year. I also work with the accounting department. I am responsible for every dollar that we take in or spend."

Baseball's AAA minor league teams see lots of players traded, moved up to the major league teams, and down to Class AA. "When a player comes down to AAA from the big leagues, he's going to be unhappy. And that usually means a full day of meetings and conference calls. The player wants to know why the team did this to him. It's a matter of pride, but also a matter of money. Suddenly he's not making, say, $100,000 or more every

"You can't really become too friendly with the players. If you get emotionally involved, it's going to be a problem."

Six-Year Free Agent List:
A major league player who has completed six years of service is eligible to be a free agent when his current contract runs out. A free agent is a player who can sign with any team.

year; he's down to the $26,000 to $40,000 range. He may no longer be on the forty-man roster. His insurance and pension situation changes. The agent is on the phone trying to get the best possible deal — the player may be upset, even angry. But now the player is our responsibility, and we have to make things work out."

When a player is sent down, this process can take several days. But when a player is called up to the majors, the Pirates want fast action. "We have to close down his apartment; we have to move him. Everything is an immediate priority. Of course, the player is so excited, he can't wait to get to the big leagues."

As the season winds down, Ken and Steve work their way through piles of paperwork and complete the year's records. Ken always goes on the final road trip of the season. "Some of the players owe us money, and we like to balance the books. I also keep an eye on our equipment and our uniforms." Until the very end, Ken looks out for the Bisons' interests. "The team means a lot to me."

After the season, Ken and the Bisons' manager review the six-year free agent list with the GM and the team's owner. "We put together a list of the players we want for the next year. The manager and I really know the players — we know what they can do — we see them more and pay more attention to the way that they play than anyone else. Then we work with the Pirates to sign the players we want. I think we take a more active role in choosing our players than a lot of other teams do."

What's next for the Lehners?

Steve is headed for college. "With eight years' experience, I don't think I'll have too much trouble finding a job after college. But there are a lot of things in this world besides baseball. We're both young, single, and willing to work anywhere baseball might take us. Even though Buffalo did not get a major league franchise, I'll probably continue with the Bisons. But there are a lot of other things that I'd like to do, too."

Ken is still optimistic about a major league baseball franchise relocating in Buffalo. "Bob's a very loyal employer, and a good one. I think he sees that there are options. He has talked about buying a major league club and moving it to Buffalo. He is head of the largest family-owned frozen food business; he tends to see good opportunities and act on them. I could be a part of the company's future. I could also move to another team, probably in the major leagues. I've made a lot of contacts, and I think I have a good reputation. But there is a whole world of opportunities beyond baseball, and like my brother says, we're both still young, still at the beginning of our careers."

Buffalo's Pilot Field, a classic neighborhood ballpark designed for easy expansion into a major league stadium.

Ken and Steve's ADVICE

"Read the box scores — familiarize yourself with what makes one player better or more valuable than another. Read your local newspaper, *USA Today, Sporting News, Baseball America,* and biographies about baseball players. Go to movies about baseball or rent the videocassettes. Get to know the business."

Steve recommends doing what he did in order to learn the game: getting involved with a team, helping out wherever you're needed. If you begin when you're in junior high, then by the time you're ready to start working part-time for a team in high school, you'll know more than most people do.

If you live in a town that has a minor league team, you can probably get your foot in the door by volunteering. Call the stadium and request a media guide; in addition to player and team information, it lists the key people in the key departments. Write a letter to the person whose job you want to learn more about. You'll probably get a reply. Volunteer to help. You may not get the job you originally envisioned, but you may be introduced to another department that needs help. The idea is to get involved with the team — to get in. You'll meet people, you'll hear about opportunities, and you'll see how the team operates.

Once you're in college, arrange for an internship. "We have over thirty interns working for the Bisons," Steve comments. "If you don't do this kind of thing, it's very hard to get started in baseball."

"It's easiest to get started in Class A or AA and work your way up," Ken advises. "But don't get discouraged — even the big league teams in New York and Los Angeles need interns and hire part-time help."

Both Ken and Steve recommend a broad-based high school and college education. "The first and most important building block is doing well at school. You must learn to communicate, to read and write effectively, to handle basic mathematics, to deal with people."

Ken is skeptical about too much college-level work in sports or sports management. "It's a relatively new major, and a lot of people do not know what it involves. I think it's better to get a liberal arts degree, maybe in communications or English, or a degree in business. You may not work in sports all your life — a degree is something you can fall back on."

Getting the first job is easier if you've done some volunteer work or an internship. Most teams tend to promote from within the organization. ∎

Umpire
ERIC GREGG

Eric Gregg is a National League umpire. He is also the author of Working the Plate: The Eric Gregg Story, *written with Marty Appel (William Morrow and Company, 1990).*

My dream was to play for the Philadelphia Phillies. That's what I wanted to do since I can remember. And until I was about fifteen, I thought I had a shot at the majors. Baseball was the most important thing in my life. I loved to watch it; I loved to play it. I could hit the ball, but at five-foot-one and about two hundred pounds, it was hard for me to beat out the fielder and get on base. I was a third-string catcher for the team at West Philadelphia High School when I heard those dreaded words from my coach, Joe Goldenberg: he said, 'Eric, I've got to be honest with you. If you can't play ball for the West Philly Speed Boys, there's no way you're gonna play for the Phillies.'"

This was not Eric's first experience with disappointment.

Eric grew up in a tough West Philadelphia neighborhood called the Bottom. "We called it the Bottom because there was no place to go but up." The neighborhood was poor, with an abundance of drug pushers and tough characters. His parents had a rough time making ends meet, and his family broke up for a while. Later his brother Ernie was convicted of selling drugs; his jail cell was firebombed, and Ernie received burns on 90 percent of his body. Eric realized

that his life was in his own hands. He did what he had to do in order to get out.

"When it came time for junior high, I was smart enough to know that the neighborhood school was trouble. Somehow, at an early age, I knew I had to get away. So all by myself, I faked my home address and enrolled at another school, one that was half black and half white. I took the bus every day. I smile and look back on it now; it was a gutsy move for a thirteen-year-old kid."

Eric delivered newspapers, shined shoes, and bussed tables in a diner to earn pocket money. In his spare time, he played baseball. He became a powerful home-run hitter, and on sheer enthusiasm alone, he figured he would make it to the majors. When the coach told him otherwise, Eric wasn't sure what he would do. Then fate intervened.

"I was sitting at home on a Saturday afternoon, watching *The Game of the Week* on NBC. During a break in the action, Curt Gowdy read an announcement from Major League Baseball. He said, 'Become a major league umpire. Make thirty thousand dollars a year. For information, write to Umpire Development School, St. Petersburg, Florida.' I sat up straight in my chair. Thirty thousand sounded like a fortune! And he did say, 'Major league.' I wrote a letter, but I was so excited that I didn't even wait for the letter to reach them. I got the number, called, and asked to speak with the person in charge. His name was Barney Deary."

At first Barney was very positive. Then he mentioned the one requirement that Eric could not meet, something he could do nothing about: the school required its applicants to be twenty-one years old! "Barney told me that he couldn't take me. But he also told me that he could arrange for me to umpire Little League games in the Philadelphia area to get me started. And that's just what he did."

Eric started his career by umpiring games played by six- and seven-year-old kids. "They taught me a lot. I remember one kid who said, on a 3–2 count, 'Mister, you see that guy coaching third base? That's my dad. I've struck out three times today, and if I strike out again, he's really gonna let me have it!' The next pitch was a strike, but it was close, so I called it a ball. The kid walked. A week later I found out that little Billy pulled the same stunt every week!"

After two years of umpiring Little League, Eric contacted Barney again, to tell him that he was certain that he wanted to be an umpire. The school's age restriction had been relaxed; a new student could now enroll at age nineteen. Since Eric would turn nineteen during the school's term, he was accepted.

"The classroom sessions were fascinating. I hadn't always been attentive in high school, but now I saw my future on the line, and I knew that it was time to pay attention or to get out. The teachers would come up with these impossible situations, just so you'd be ready for anything. And I was a great student. High school had been a struggle, but here I was picking up everything first shot out of the box. It was amazing."

At umpire school, students play mock baseball games. Eric learned about the importance of timing and about positioning himself so he could see the play, and he developed the ability to withstand verbal abuse. "The teachers would attack you right to your face, and see whether you'd take it or run them out of the game. They were looking for character, for the right stuff." Eric finished second in his class. At age nineteen, he knew that he wanted his life's work to be umpiring.

Graduating from umpire school does not guarantee a job, however. Most people who graduate from umpire school never make the majors; many never get beyond a low-level assignment in the minor leagues.

Eric started in the New York–Penn League, umpiring Class A ball. With partner Josh Magidson, he learned the trade by traveling to small towns like Batavia, Newark (New York), Oneonta, Auburn, Erie, and Watertown. "In Oneonta, we asked where the umpires' changing room was located, and we were told to change behind the grass by the duck pond."

Over the winter, Eric found out that his contract had been optioned by the National League. This was unusual; even most umpires working in the Class AAA leagues were not under option. Here was Eric, a nineteen-year-old umpire with just one short season's experience in a very minor league, gaining recognition in the major leagues. He still isn't sure why it happened — was it his color or his talent? Eric does not worry about such things; he just keeps moving.

As a result of the option, Eric worked at major league spring training the following year. He was assigned to work with Augie Donatelli and Shag Crawford, two umpires with considerable major league experience, two of the best in the business. "It was a wonderful experience to get a taste of the majors."

That season, Eric worked the Florida State League, also umpiring Class A ball, but for a longer season than before. "It was really nice. We played in major league facilities — the ones that were built for spring training. There was hot water, good lighting in the ballparks — very different from what I had experienced before. I was the first black umpire in the league. The next year, Eric was assigned to work the Eastern League, Class AA ball, in Maryland, Pennsylvania, Connecticut, New York, and Ontario, Canada. He worked winter ball in the Dominican Republic, and moved up to Class AAA in the Pacific Coast League the following year. In just four years, Eric had moved through the minor leagues. He waited for his chance to be a major league umpire.

"I got the first call during the next season. The supervisor of National League umpires, Fred Flagg, called and asked me to work a game in Cincinnati on September 25, 1975. That was the year of the Big Red Machine in Cincinnati. And it was the night that they claimed the pennant. I was in heaven — I couldn't call enough people to tell them how great it had been to be an umpire at that game."

The following year, Eric continued in the Pacific Coast League but was called up to the majors with increasing frequency as a substitute. "Guys would take off for weddings or graduations, or they'd get sick for a few days, and I'd work in their place. The next year, on May 20, I got the call from Mr. Flagg. He told me that I was needed in San Francisco. I was the league's swing person. The next year, I started as a regular member of a four-man crew, moving from one team's home stand to the next."

Still in his mid-twenties, Eric was always the youngest, least experienced member of the crew. "I kept my mouth shut, I did the job, and they took care of me. You've got to learn to listen. And when you do, you learn a whole lot."

Eric typically starts his day at about 9:30 A.M. Breakfast consists of coffee and a bran muffin. "I'm counting calories. I'm down to eighteen hundred calories per day, dinner included." Then he takes a good hearty walk for an hour or more. He picks up lunch on the way back to his room; usually, it's a chef's salad and a couple of diet colas from a fast food restaurant. "I make sure I'm back by twelve-thirty for *The Young and the Restless*. I've been watching that show for years — I've actually been on it as a guest, and we named our daughter after Ashley Abbott. I also watch *Another World* and *Days of Our Lives*. If I'm working a night game, I try to take a nap for an hour or two in the late afternoon. I get to the ballpark by about six. The first thing I do is head for the trainer to get my ankle taped up — I broke it eight years ago, and I keep it in good shape. I'm usually the first one at the stadium. I'm part of a crew of four umpires: me, Jerry Crawford, Tom Hallion, and the crew chief, Doug Harvey. If I'm working home plate, which

"I kept my mouth shut, I did the job, and they took care of me. You've got to learn to listen. And when you do, you learn a whole lot."

Eric Gregg checks out a close play.

Umpire

Two umpiring schools share an especially good reputation:

Joe Brinkman Umpire School (1021 Indian River Drive, Cocoa, FL 32922) is a program that begins each January and ends in early February. Thirteen professional umpires teach a five- to six-week course; Brinkman is a well-known American League umpire. Students work hard — roughly seventy to eighty hours per week.

Harry Wendelstedt School for Umpires (88 South St. Andrews Drive, Ormand Beach, FL 32074) is held at the same time. Wendelstedt, a National League umpire and crew chief, supervises a staff of professional umpires, many from the major leagues.

Tuition for each school is in the $1,500 to $2,000 range.

Fifty of the best graduates from umpiring schools are invited to the Major League Baseball Umpire Development Program. After ten days of evaluation, candidates are either assigned to jobs in short-season Class A leagues or a rookie league or are placed on a reserve list and assigned when jobs become available.

Every umpire must know the rules — before you apply

I do every fourth day, I don't talk at all before the game. I need to concentrate.

"People think umpiring is an easy job. They're wrong. It's a stressful job and a thankless one. When people say it's easy, they don't understand what an umpire does. We must watch every play, we must be sure that we see it clearly, and we must make a decision instantly."

His most famous game, described in detail in his book, *Working the Plate,* was played at Chicago's Wrigley Field on August 17 and 18, 1982. The Cubs got a run in the first, the Dodgers tied it in the second, and a pitching duel froze that score until the eighth inning. Larry Bowa singled for Chicago. Leon Durham belted a double, and Bowa headed home. In a close play, Eric called him out. "It was a one-inch play in a cloud of dust: a question of whether someone got his toe through the catcher's leg or not." Eric was sure that he was right. The Cubs' manager, who could not possibly have seen the play from his position in the dugout, argued heatedly, as did Bowa, but Eric didn't change his call. Nine more innings were played before the game had to be called on account of darkness (this was before Wrigley had lights).

"We were back at the ballpark the next day to resume play in the eighteenth inning. I was dead tired, and we had a regularly scheduled game to follow the completion of the suspended game."

The game ended with another play at the plate. The Dodgers' Steve Sax was headed for home. "There was another cloud of dust. My right arm started to go up — my elbow was bent. But then my baseball instincts took over, the instincts that tell you after those thousands of games whether the play is safe or out. Quickly my arms flattened, and I yelled, '*Safe!*'"

When the inning was over, Eric ran for cover. Some fans scaled the wall, and he thought they were after him. Cubs announcer Harry Caray suggested on the air that Eric had made the wrong call. ESPN said flat out that he had blown it. Eric called it "a tough day at the office," shook it off, and got to work on the second game of the day. Thankfully, there were no problems in that game.

After most games, Eric heads back to the hotel room and switches on ESPN's *Sports Center*. "I like to see how the other umpires did. I watch for the controversial plays because I always learn from them. Sometimes, I'll go out for a bite with the other umpires on my crew or with people we know in the city that we're visiting. It's a great life, but I miss my family when I'm on the road, and during the season, I'm on the road most of the time."

Happily married, Eric lives in the Philadelphia area. On the field, he's a colorful guy, an umpire who's fun to watch (he once danced with the Philly Phanatic, for example). Off the field, he is becoming a celebrity. He speaks at a lot of banquets: fund-raisers for civic organizations and charities. Frequently, he appears with major sports celebrities, some of whom have become good friends of his.

His dream of writing a book someday came true sooner than expected. "An agent in New York who had represented Tom Seaver, Dwight Gooden, and some other well-known players, heard that I was a good dinner speaker. When we met, we talked about how well Ron Luciano had done writing books about his life as an umpire, and I decided it was worth a try." Through the agent, Eric met Marty Appel, who had written several baseball biographies. They worked together for several days and developed a book proposal, filled mostly with baseball stories. The publishers, as it turned out, wanted something different — they wanted more autobiographical material, including details about his early years in the Bottom. "At first I wasn't sure I wanted to do that. My dad was very much against it. Then I figured if I can help even one kid who came from my kind of background, it would be worth doing. I know I made the right decision."

Eric has appeared on radio talk shows in just about every major league city to promote the book. He has also appeared on several network television programs, including *The Today Show*.

to umpire school, watch a lot of games, ask questions, and commit this book to memory: *The Sporting News Official Baseball Rules Handbook* (about $2.00). Write to: *Sporting News,* P.O. Box 56, St. Louis, MO 63166.

Umpire

Eric's ADVICE

"Start out by volunteering to umpire T-ball. That would be your first exposure to people screaming at you — moms and dads calling you names. You might be turned off by it, or you might find out that you can handle it. It's a good idea to umpire for kids who are younger than you are. Get in touch with some baseball coaches in your area — they'll be able to put you in contact with local baseball associations. There is *always* a need for umpires. You'll earn money, too, probably ten or fifteen dollars per game for younger kids, maybe as much as twenty-five dollars or so for older ones.

"Being an umpire for Little League games also forces discipline — you must learn the entire rule book, and you must make the correct decision in a split second. When you're fourteen or fifteen, you can start attending clinics for umpires. Some of these clinics are run by professional umpires who work in the minor leagues, and even in the major leagues."

Throughout junior high and high school, pay attention to grades. "I didn't go to college because I didn't have the grades. Don't make that mistake — it limits your options. There are only twenty-four umpires in the National League, twenty-eight in the American League, and about six guys on option. You can work in the minors, but you won't make much money, even in AAA ball. You can work part-time as an umpire at high school games; you can play either on a formal team or for fun. And the more games you see, the more you are a part of baseball, the more your skills will improve.

"Get your strike motion together — figure out why you missed a play — why weren't you kneeling, why weren't you paying attention? You have to learn how to keep your cool. You also have to learn when to toss a guy; it's better to get a guy out too quickly to show that you're the boss than it is to toss five out later. Talk to the coach — tell him if he can't control the team, then you will. Try, above all, to keep the players playing the game. When a player screams at you, he knows that you're not going to change your call, but he's hoping that you'll be more lenient on the next call. You can get that kind of experience only by working the game."

To become an umpire, you must attend an umpiring school. "If you're good, you'll get assigned to a Class A league. But don't get married until you reach at least AAA ball — you'll be making very little money, and you'll be moving every year for at least five years as you work your way up (or out)." ■

Media Relations Director
SHARON PANNOZZO

I n major league baseball, the media relations department does much more than work with the press. Most people are surprised at the amount of statistics involved, for example. We keep records on every player, every game, and every play. We supply this information to the press, and we recalculate these statistics regularly for use in the yearbook and in the media guide, which our department prepares every year. We also run the press booth and supply every reporter with game notes they can use to write their stories.

"In addition, we're the official team spokespeople; if the team trades a player, we make the announcement. We prepare press releases and send them out. In the off-season, we run a hot stove luncheon tour with players, and we travel throughout the Midwest. When someone calls to find out what number was on the uniform of a Cub who played second base in the early 1930s, we find the answer. We handle press credentials — when a member of the press wants access to the stadium, we determine who gets in and who does not. We arrange press

Sharon Pannozzo is the director of media relations for the Chicago Cubs.

interviews with the players and the manager. We arrange for spokespeople — the Special Olympics, for example, wanted an official Chicago spokesperson, so we recommended Mitch Williams when he was with the team, because he loves kids. I guess that's the short list."

When Sharon was eleven years old, living in western Massachusetts in the small town of Lee (population 7,000), she had no intention of becoming a major league public relations executive. She wanted to be a lawyer. "It was probably because I thought that all lawyers made lots and lots of money. Then I realized that they also had to work hard and that a lot of their work was research. I figured, even when I was that young, that anything I was going to do for my adult life was going to have to be fun. Being a lawyer didn't sound like much fun, so I decided I wanted to be a nuclear physicist — I think I liked the sound of that. Then I visited a plant and decided that didn't look like much fun either."

She wasn't much of a sports fan, though she did occasionally watch the Red Sox on television. And she wasn't much of an athlete, though she did catch for a girls' softball team in junior high school.

In high school, she talked her way into a writing job with a small community newspaper. "They were willing to pay me a dollar per column inch [a column inch is one inch of a column of newspaper text], so I wrote my stories as long as possible! I usually wrote about high school football, because I was a cheerleader and I had to travel to all of the games anyway. I always wrote nice things about the guys on the team."

As she gained more experience, Sharon became more comfortable with the idea of a career in sports journalism. She even thought she could do a better job than one of the few female sports journalists on network TV at the time, Phyllis George. She began to take her intentions seriously and researched colleges that offered a sports journalism degree. She decided on the University of Massachusetts (UMass) at Amherst, because it offered the degree and was only about ninety minutes from home.

The first year, she took some core courses and then got the news that UMass was doing away with her major! Fortunately, the school also changed the level of the sports *management* program from graduate to undergrad. It was a lucky break. Sharon's course work became more diverse, and ultimately, it was more useful than classes in sports journalism alone would have been. "I took courses in sports marketing, facilities management, the history of sports, the psychology of sports, and even the philosophy of sports. I also had minors — I tried to make myself as well rounded as possible. I took a lot of courses in marketing, journalism, communications, and physical education. I loved school — the program was great for me. In addition to the course work, I worked for the director of sports information. I kept score at the football games, kept defensive stats, copied post-game notes, and even called the papers after the games."

Heading into her senior year, Sharon began to realize the obstacles facing women who want careers in the business of professional sports. "This is not just a preconceived notion on my part. It's a professional reality. I really wanted to work in football, but the field is just not accessible to women. As it happened, though, an opportunity did open up for me in baseball. My school's sports information director was friendly with the director of public relations for the Red Sox. He had gone to UMass, and I met him at an alumni event. In fact, he took me to dinner, and a short time later, he asked me to come in for an interview, and I became an intern for the team. It was a big deal — the Red Sox had never hired an intern before.

"So I started working in public relations. They paid only my gas money, and I lived with a relative in Boston so I didn't have to pay any rent. I worked every day from January until June and got a taste of the work both off-season and during the season. Early on, I spent a lot of time putting facts together for the media guide and taking care of correspondence. When the season began, I helped

"I really wanted to work in football, but the field is just not accessible to women."

Media Relations Director

with the game notes and the stats, and, like all interns, I spent a lot of time at the copy machine and answering phones."

After the internship, Sharon graduated and started looking for a job. "I interviewed for a few assistant SID (sports information director) positions, but I guess I really wasn't serious about finding a job. I decided to get an M.B.A. at Boston University, but before I started, I heard through friends at the Red Sox that there had been a shake-up at the Cubs' public relations office and there were jobs open. This was a Tuesday; I found out that they needed someone to start on Friday. I called, and they told me that they couldn't fly me to Chicago, that they had already flown in too many people. I told them I'd be there on Friday. After making arrangements to stay the weekend in Chicago, I left Boston on Thursday afternoon, drove through the night, and arrived at 9:00 A.M. on Friday, after getting totally lost in an unfamiliar city. I spent the entire day talking to people in the department. In between interviews, I helped label envelopes. They had me write a sample press release; they took me to lunch. And all the time, I'm exhausted — I haven't slept since Wednesday night. Anyway, I left at five o'clock on Friday night and told them that I could stay and start on Monday but that they had to make a decision. I was planning to drive back to Boston late in the day on Saturday. They called me Saturday morning and said, 'The job is yours!'"

Sharon worked in Chicago through the following week, drove back to Boston the next weekend to collect her belongings, and has lived in Chicago ever since.

"I'm starting my ninth season with the Cubs. And I'm happy to say that I recently completed my M.B.A. at Northwestern University."

She travels with the team. "Don Zimmer treats me like a daughter. I'm

Sharon watches a game from the press booth.

not just some woman hanging around. I'm on the bus or the plane with the players. Sometimes a new player will look at me strangely, but that's not happening as often as it once did. Most people understand what I do, and how important it is to the team's operation.

"I think going out during the winter to banquets really helps a lot. We run three buses and do two-day tours, stopping in one city in the Midwest for lunch and another for dinner. We take three or four players, a broadcaster who acts as emcee, and someone from the front office. Local organizations sponsor these events and use them to make money for themselves. It's great public relations for us, and it helps with group ticket sales. I organize a lot of them — I'm the chief baby-sitter, the person who talks the players into coming along, who wakes people up when we're on the road. It's a lot of fun once we're there, but it's also a lot of work. The players do it because they want to give something back to the community. They sign autographs, give little speeches, take pictures with fans and local dignitaries, and do interviews with the local press. On one trip to Rockford, Illinois, Mike Bielecki, Shawon Dunston, Lloyd McClendon, and Jim Frey, our general manager, went along. In just one place, we can see more than a thousand fans."

Sharon works long hours but says that's normal for baseball and for most professional sports. Salaries are low, but the job comes with some prestige — and a lot of excitement. Sharon hopes to make her way further into management, to move up a few levels and eventually oversee all of the team's marketing and financial operations. She plans to stay in baseball, but she is "definitely keeping an eye out for changes in pro football." There are not yet any women in pro football management, but then, somebody's got to be the first.

Lingo

Press Release:
A one- to two-page news story about a person or an event that is distributed to radio and television stations, magazines, and newspapers. Reporters use the information in the press release to write the story or as background for an interview.

M.B.A.:
Master's in business administration, a business degree granted by graduate schools.

Emcee:
The word is the sounded-out form of M.C., which is short for master of ceremonies — someone who serves as the host of an event.

Sharon's ADVICE

"My younger sister just started as a marketing assistant for the Boston Red Sox. She's followed in my footsteps, with the same SID job at UMass and the same Red Sox internship. But things will probably be easier for her — things are changing, even if it is slowly, and there will be more opportunities for women in professional sports."

Whether you're male or female, Sharon insists that "you really have to like sports to do this job. You are going to watch over a hundred games a year. It's easy to grow tired of it. But it's not enough just to like sports — you really need to understand the game. Learn to keep score. And I think there's a lot to be said for collecting baseball cards and for talking endlessly about which player is better, who's the best second baseman in the league, that kind of thing. If you really want to get into it, even at a young age, start keeping a score book, and work on your stats. It's also a good idea to read the sports pages every day to get to know what's happening."

Once you're in junior high or high school, get to know the professional sports organizations in your area. If there's a minor league team nearby, try to get involved. Offer to work in the office for free. If you're dependable, you'll get plenty to do. "I worked for the Holyoke Millers. I did the team's laundry, I made sno-cones, I counted the ticket sales at the end of each game. We were an Eastern League Class A team for the Brewers."

Also, write for the local newspaper. "Get yourself a beat — covering every game at your high school, for example. You can learn a lot by writing about a sport. Even more important, you'll learn how to build professional relationships."

Sharon insists on college. "Learn how to write. A communications or a journalism degree is fine. A sports management degree may prove too specific — there are not a lot of jobs in professional sports."

The Cubs will not hire you unless you have a college degree. And Sharon will not hire you unless you have done an internship with a professional team, preferably a major league baseball team. "The Cubs now have internship programs in every department, even accounting. We regularly hire former interns. Baseball is a very tight-knit industry. It is very, very hard to find a job, period. Without that internship, you're only making it harder on yourself. And internships are not hard to get. Usually the school sets it up, but you can write a letter yourself. We'll interview you, and if you're bright and you're willing to work hard, you'll get in as an intern. What you're able to do from there is up to you." ■

Ticket Operations Director
RICHARD DEATS

P eople have the impression that on Opening Day, 50,000 fans magically appear outside the stadium. Where did all of those people come from? Obviously, a lot of them bought tickets long before April 10, but that's not what most people think when they see the crowd."

Despite his official-sounding title, Richard Deats makes his job description clear to anyone who asks: "Basically, I'm in charge of selling tickets." A lot of them. In a good season, Richard and his staff sell over two million tickets — about average for a major league team in a big city. "You're only as good as your team. When the Phillies finish last two years in a row, like they did a few years ago, ticket sales are going to be down. But when we have a good year, we can go as high as three million." Unfortunately, Veterans Stadium has 60,000 seats, so even in a good year, there are a lot of empty sections during each game. "The stadium was built in the 1970s as a multipurpose arena where football and other sports could be played. The stadiums they're building now are for baseball only, and they have about 45,000 seats. That's a good number for baseball.

"Advance sales are really the name of the game. We're lucky because we have 16,000 season-ticket holders, so even before the season

Richard Deats is vice president of sales and ticket operations for the Philadelphia Phillies.

starts, we have about 1.3 million seats sold." The other one million or so are sold to individuals who buy in advance or on the day of the game or to groups of twenty-five or more.

Thirty years ago, most of the seats at the ballpark were sold to walk-ups — people who walked over to the stadium on the day of the game to buy a ticket. This is still possible in some cities, where the ballpark is in the center of a busy business district, but Veterans Stadium, like so many of the newer parks, is on the edge of town, mainly accessible only by car. On a big night, like a weekend night in July when fireworks are scheduled to follow the game, the Phillies can sell as many as 10,000 tickets to walk-ups. But on a cold night in April or September, there may be only five hundred walk-ups.

The other seats are sold through direct marketing, by mail and phone. Richard and his staff refer to the Phillies as their product and to unsold tickets as inventory. "We maintain a mailing list of more than 200,000 names and addresses. All of the names on the list have sampled our product in the past. They've bought tickets in the past, or bought a Philly Phanatic doll and sent us back the information card that we include with each one, or brought a business or church group to the stadium, or just asked for information." During the off-season, Richard's marketing staff prepares a mailing for some or all of the names on the list. The mailing goes out before the season begins and is supported by advertisements on television and radio.

Under Richard's leadership, the Phillies have developed one of the most sophisticated ticket management systems in the major leagues. The club has its own computer system, and when a fan calls to order tickets, a member of Richard's staff can immediately call up the best available seats in each price range. The system can also recommend seats to fans with specific requirements such as wanting to sit in the shade or in the first row of a section. During the busiest part of the season, as many as eighteen people work the phones. "Some teams farm this out to a Ticketmaster or a

Ticketron service. We do the work ourselves, although we do also make tickets available through those other services
for the fans' convenience. It's cheaper
to buy directly from us, because we
don't add a service charge." The computer system has worked so well for the
Phillies that it is now used by the Philadelphia Eagles (the football team that
shares Veterans Stadium); it has been
adapted for use by the Philadelphia Zoo
as well.

Richard's ticket sales operation
is heavily dependent upon
computers.

Many seats are also sold to groups,
including church organizations, busi-
ness offices, schools, and camps. Richard sees group sales as a
marketing tool: "We want people to think about the ballpark as a
fun place to spend their leisure time. A lot of the people who come
with groups might not buy tickets on their own. But once they're
in the park and they have a good time, they become potential
customers for individual sales later in the season."

When Richard was young, he had no special plans to work in
professional sports. "I played baseball, football, and basketball —
plenty of Little League. Sports, particularly baseball, was always
the thing I liked best. I was a decent hitter; I played third and the
outfield. I was also a big reader — I read everything, the Hardy
Boys stories, Robert Louis Stevenson, and of course, a lot about
sports.

"In college, I wanted to play football and baseball and get a good
education. I applied to Colgate and the University of Pennsylvania. I was realistic — I knew I wasn't going to be a professional
player, but I was good enough to play on some college teams."

Richard went to Penn, became a history major, and found his
first job as a physical education teacher at a private school,
Germantown Academy, outside Philadelphia. He taught elemen-

"You must understand that the Phillies, like most baseball clubs, is a small company. Everybody in the front office knows everybody else, and when jobs open up, the club usually hires and promotes from within."

tary school and also coached the high school teams. "It was great to teach young kids phys. ed., to get them to use their energy, their muscles. I really liked the job."

While working at Germantown, Richard was always on the lookout for a summer job. "I got to know Robin Roberts [a Phillies pitching legend and a Hall of Famer] because his children attended the Academy. And through Robin, I got to know Bill Giles [then the Phillies executive vice president, now the owner], who hired me to work part-time during the off-season, selling tickets by phone."

Through that season, Richard worked as a ticket seller. "A lot of teachers work in baseball during the summer. The schedules match up beautifully."

After four years of teaching, Richard realized that he was going to need a larger salary — he was starting a family. He heard about an opening at the Phillies as an assistant ticket office manager. Through his summer work, he knew the people and how the ticket office worked. He was the logical choice for the job.

"I worked as an assistant for two years. Then the director of group sales left, and I took over his position. Later, when Bill Giles and his partners bought the Phillies, David Montgomery, the director of ticket sales, moved up into Bill's old job, and I moved up into his position.

"You must understand that the Phillies, like most baseball clubs, is a small company. Everybody in the front office knows everybody else, and when jobs open up, the club usually hires and promotes from within. That's the way most clubs work. There's a strong feeling of family here — we all spend a lot of hours working here, so we all get to know one another pretty well." With talent and patience, and a lot of long hours and hard work, Richard has become an important member of the management team behind the Phillies' success.

Richard Deats: A Typical Day

"I wish I had a typical day, but there's really no such thing in this business. At the beginning of a game day, I doublecheck the status of tickets from last night's game. I check the number of tickets sold, the number remaining, and make sure that those numbers match up with our attendance figures. Usually, we'll have a staff meeting about an upcoming home stand or a promotion that's coming up. If we're headed for a busy weekend, we might talk about hiring extra ticket sellers or extra people on the phone lines."

Richard's afternoon may be spent in several different ways. "Sometimes, I just return phone calls. Or I may have to make some special preparation for the game day — for a group that might be coming in, for example. Most of what I do is managerial — I make sure that the whole machine works properly. I also work on long-range projects, such as expanding the phone center or making plans for the following season.

"I stay for the night's game. In most cases, once the game begins, we work out the attendance figure, match that against the turnstile count, and add the complimentary tickets. There are also some financial statements to be prepared. A percentage of the gate — money from ticket sales — goes to the visiting team and to the league office.

"During the winter, my hours are nine to five. We're preparing for the upcoming season: collecting payment from last year's season-ticket holders and selling new season tickets. From the operations end, we're ordering new ticket stock, updating our computer systems, and working with advance sales to individuals and groups.

"The first goal is to sell tickets. The second goal is to collect the money. The third is to print and produce the tickets. That's the short story of what the sales department does, day in and day out."

Richard's ADVICE

"There's a real difference between the baseball side and the business side. On the business side, we are promoting a product. Our product may be special and unique, but all of the other aspects of our business are the same as in any other business. Like any other company, we have a sales department, an accounting department, and so on. The big difference on a sports team is what businesses call product development — our scouts must have baseball-related skills. And the same is true of the coaches, manager, trainers, and other people. But in sales and marketing, an interest in baseball is really secondary to a good business background."

Richard sees the development of leadership and communications skills as vitally important to success in the front office. And the best way to build those skills, according to Richard, is a solid education.

"When you're a teenager, get to know what's going on in sports, but don't limit your scope." If the idea of marketing interests you, learn more about what marketing means by getting out and talking to some people who do it for a living. If you live in a minor league town, volunteer to work in the ticket office, and you'll get a solid education in baseball marketing from the ground up.

As for college, Richard recommends a marketing degree, *if* that's your strong suit. "Don't try to bend your personality to a major. Instead, major in what interests you — if you want a job like mine, you'll find that a degree in accounting or sports management will be useful." Bear in mind, however, that Richard's degree is in history; the subject studied isn't nearly as important as the fact that you have a degree — that you've completed college and that you are both interested in baseball and capable of working your way up. "Spend your free time working for a local team; part-time employees are the ones who are most likely to get the jobs when full-time positions become available.

"I hesitate to tell someone to prepare for a career in pro sports. There are only twenty-six major league baseball teams, and only twenty-six jobs like mine. Think about the minor leagues — think about other sports. Don't just focus on major league baseball — you may be disappointed." ∎

Clubhouse Manager
IAN DUFF

Ian Duff is the visiting clubhouse manager for the Toronto Blue Jays.

For a day game, the first thing I'll do is stop and pick up a few dozen doughnuts for the clubhouse. Then I might go to a twenty-four-hour grocery store for cold cuts, fruit, toothpaste, and anything else that we might need. I guess you could say that I run a combination hotel, variety store, shoe shine stand, laundry, restaurant, and a lot of other things, too."

Welcome to the visiting team clubhouse for the Toronto Blue Jays. Located in the basement level of the new Skydome in downtown Toronto, this is the place where visiting clubhouse manager Ian Duff spends all day and much of the night throughout baseball season.

"I'm usually one of the first people to get to the stadium — I arrive at about 8:00 A.M. for a day game. I'll make the coffee and make sure that the night crew did a good job of cleaning up. If they didn't, I see that the job gets done. Then my assistant and I put the players' uniforms into their lockers and check stock on soft drinks, fruit juices, candy bars, yogurt, and dry cereal. And then we fold towels." Ian supervises a small staff, including the bat boys, whose jobs entail helping out in the Blue Jays' and visitors' clubhouses.

The players, coaches, and trainers start arriving by about 9:00 A.M. "McDonald's has the concession for food here at the Skydome, so players often ask for

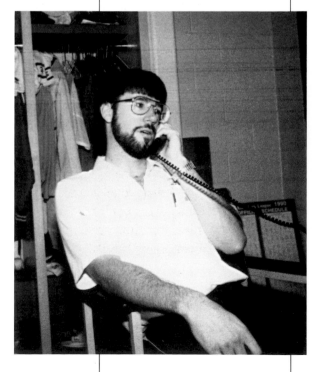

something, and I send one of my assistants to get an Egg McMuffin or a burger."

Ian's busy time is during the hour or two before batting practice. The Texas Rangers are in town. Their trainer has run out of plastic bags. Ian has a box in his storeroom. A player wants to read and relax with a magazine. Ian has cartons full; he tells the player to take his choice. A player needs to rent a tuxedo for an event after the game. Ian asks for the player's measurements and makes arrangements for the tuxedo to be delivered. Batteries? Ian stocks all of the usual sizes. Shampoo? Mouthwash? Deodorant? Chewing tobacco? Name your brand. Brushes, combs, piks. Ian's office even provides music for the clubhouse. One player requests something deep and soulful. A few minutes later, someone asks for Clint Black. "Man, he was the country singer of the year last year — you gotta get some of his stuff." It's hard to satisfy everyone.

During batting practice, Ian washes a load of towels. He spends some time in his office checking arrangements for a delivery, ordering more supplies by phone, and waiting for the players to return to the clubhouse. This is also an hour when Ian and his staff can relax a bit, maybe watch a little of the batting practice.

As the players change out of their workout clothes, piles of laundry grow on the clubhouse floor. Ian and his assistants pick up the clothes, toss them into carts, and take care of business. "We probably do at least a dozen loads a day." Ian smiles. Laundry is part of the job; he doesn't especially mind it. He's also meticulous: "I don't like to see dirty towels lying around."

As the players change for the game, there are last-minute problems. One player forgot to reserve tickets for a relative; another hoped to return to the hotel to pack but ran out of time; a third needs two hundred U.S. dollars exchanged for Canadian dollars. Ian takes care of these details. "A few years ago, Reggie Jackson was in. He had a six-hundred-page manuscript for his book, and he needed us to make a copy. We pick up suits that a player ordered. We arrange golf dates on off-days, dinner reservations, places to go after the game. It's always something different."

Game time. The players leave the clubhouse. Ian and his staff vacuum and tidy things up. A load of laundry is ready to come out of the machines; underwear, jocks, and workout clothes are hung up to dry. Ian sets up the back room for the post-game meal.

"By about the fourth or fifth inning, my assistant goes to get the food. A few of us watch an inning or two of the game, or play cards, or lie down and relax." By the eighth inning, the laundry carts are in place, ready for dirty towels and uniforms.

"We always pay attention to the last out. If the visiting team lost, we make sure the TVs and radios are off. Five minutes after the game is over, reporters come into the clubhouse for interviews." That goes on for up to a half hour, as players are showering and getting into street clothes. Ian and his staff spend the time picking up dirty laundry. They also pick up, clean, and polish each player's spiked baseball shoes. "The players are not really expected to do anything besides play the game. We take care of their needs."

Within an hour after game time, the visiting team's bus leaves, and most of the players are gone. A few have their own plans after the game and leave by private car or cab. "When the team clears out, we get to work. There are three loads of laundry for uniforms and three more for underwear and the like. It takes almost three hours to put it all away." In addition, there's cleanup after the team's meal and more vacuuming and tidying up. "We like to finish everything before we leave for home. You never know what will be facing you the next morning."

Ian Duff and his staff are responsible for the care of visiting players, including laundering their uniforms.

After a busy twelve-hour day, Ian and his crew must wait for the next visiting team's equipment to arrive in Toronto, then unpack it and prepare for the next game. Sometimes he stays at the stadium for forty-eight hours at a stretch.

Every three or four days, Ian and his staff are host to a new visiting team. On this particular night, the Texas Rangers have completed their series with Toronto, so all of their uniforms and equipment must be packed up, ready to be sent with the team that night as they head to the next town and the next ballpark. For a day game, this means that Ian finishes work by eight or nine at night. More often, the last game is a night game, which means that Ian and his staff stay until 2:00 A.M. or later.

"It's worse when we have to unpack an incoming team on the same night." In some other city, another clubhouse crew has packed up another team's equipment and sent it on a truck to the airport with the team. After a busy twelve-hour day, Ian and his crew must wait for the next visiting team's equipment to arrive in Toronto, then unpack it and prepare for the next game. Sometimes he stays at the stadium for as long as forty-eight hours at a stretch. "But it isn't usually all that bad. And it's worse for teams that can be rained out — at least with the Skydome, we know we're going to play the game regardless of the weather and there won't be any delays."

Still, Ian's not complaining. "It's fantasyland. It's not like a real job. The work is definitely hard, but it's not like sitting in an office with a suit on all day. It's exciting — things are always happening here.

"When I was growing up, I hoped to be in music, television, or professional sports. I suppose a lot of people have those dreams. Now that I'm actually doing it every day, I see that it's not all fun and games, but I can also see how different this is from an ordinary job."

Ian remains a fan, even though he works with well-known baseball players day in and day out. "I enjoy the opportunity to meet a George Brett or a Nolan Ryan and to develop a relationship, not just with the baseball player but with the person — to sit down and have a drink with them, to talk and relax with them."

He has even met President Bush. "The Texas franchise is partially owned by George Bush's son. When Texas was here for the first game of the season, George Bush and our prime minister, Brian Mulroney, threw out the first ball at the same time. I got my picture taken with both of them."

Ian has also spent some time with other celebrities. "A lot of celebrities admire baseball players, so we have famous people in the clubhouse from time to time. I've gotten friendly with some of the guys in the rock band Rush, and the lead from *Les Miserables* sang the anthem for us a few times, so some friends and I went to see his show and visited him backstage. I spent an evening with a Hollywood actor named Ed Lauter, who was a friend of Dick Howser. We were sitting around until three in the morning, telling show business and baseball stories. I've also worked a few games in other sports, so I've gotten to meet some of the 76ers and Pistons, as well as some of the professional tennis players, like McEnroe, Lendl, and Sampras."

Ian doesn't have much of a social life when the Blue Jays are playing at home — he usually works fourteen hours a day or more. But he does get a break when the team goes on the road. "When the Blue Jays are on the road, I'm still concerned with packing up the last team we saw or getting ready for the one that will be coming in for the next home stand, but I do sometimes get a chance to relax, play golf, travel, or go off to my friend's cottage."

During the winter, he enjoys spending time with friends and family. He also skis as often as possible. And he looks forward to the team's annual spring training in Dunedin, Florida. "We spend about two months down there, from the second week in February until the first week in April. It's just in time to miss the biggest snowstorms and to beat the winter blues in Toronto."

When Ian was eleven and twelve, his father was the airport manager for British Airways in Montreal. "At first, I wanted to join

Stocking Up

Ian is in charge of ordering food and supplies for both the Blue Jays and the visiting clubhouse. In a typical season, here's most of what he orders:

• 5 cases of peanut butter (12 jars per case)
• 18 cases of peanut butter and crackers (48 per case)
• 18 cases of cheese and crackers (48 per case)
• 5,600 one-pint containers of milk
• 4,000 one-pint containers of chocolate milk
• 12 cases of coffee
• 900 cases of soda (24 cans per case)
• 600 cases of fruit juice (24 cans per case)
• 140 cases of potato chips and similar snacks (52 bags per case)
• 60 dozen containers of yogurt
• 500 large cans of soup
• 200 large boxes of cereal
• 6 cases of raisins (small boxes)
• 10 cases of almonds (small boxes)
• 15 cases of Crispy Squares (crisped rice with marshmallows)
• 24 cases of Kraft Lunchables (quick sandwiches)
• 20 jars of mayonnaise
• 80 jars of jam

the Air Force to learn to fly, figuring maybe I'd become a pilot, but as I read about the music industry, entertainment sounded more exciting, more glamorous." Meanwhile, Ian played some baseball, hockey, and soccer. He was an average athlete, so he did not foresee a playing career.

His dad was transferred to Toronto when Ian was thirteen. By then, Ian was the associate director of his high school drama program, doing set construction and lighting and involved in just about all aspects of production. "We finished second in the province's theater festival. I still remember the rush — I was onstage, and the audience really responded to something I did. That's when I got really interested in theater, television, and the entertainment industry."

Ian had a friend named John Robulack in high school, and both of them were interested in baseball. Specifically, they were interested in getting season tickets if, and when, the San Francisco Giants moved to Toronto. "We were at the Canadian National Exhibition — a big national fair — and at one of the tents, the Giants had a table with literature." A short time later, the Giants deal fell apart, but Toronto became an American League expansion city. "John and I decided that no matter what, we were going to become season-ticket holders. We went downtown to put our names on the list — but we found out that there were about 6,000 people ahead of us, so we probably weren't going to get very good seats. We tried to meet the ticket manager, to convince him that we should have better seats. We dropped by the office a few times a week, and we'd talk to the receptionist, Mary Murdy, and to some of the people who worked there. It got to a point where people would ask us to deliver packages for them — they started to trust us."

The ticket office needed help stuffing envelopes and mailing out season tickets, in fact. "They asked us to help. They paid us twenty dollars. And we kept dropping by the offices.

"In the December before the first Blue Jays season, Peter Bavasi, the team's president, took us aside and said, 'You're obviously baseball fans. Why don't you work for us?' In three seconds we said, '*Yes!!!*'"

Ian joined up in time to travel to Florida for spring training as the assistant to the equipment manager. His friend John became the visiting clubhouse manager's assistant. "I was unhappy with my college situation — I hadn't gotten into the theater program to which I had applied. I ended up leaving early."

Ian stayed on as the assistant to John Silverman, the Blue Jays' equipment man, for three years. For the fourth year, he assisted Jeff Ross, who replaced John when he left for a similar job in Montreal. Jeff took over the home clubhouse the next year, and Ian took over the visiting clubhouse, his present position. (Ian's friend John Robulack, incidentally, stayed for over two years and left to become an architect. John considers Ian to be the lucky one.)

Ian has been visiting clubhouse manager for a decade. "My only real option now is to take over Jeff's job in the Blue Jays' clubhouse; that's the only job that really interests me here. I don't think I'd like to move into the front office — this is far more interesting to me." Ian's opportunities in Canada are limited — the Expos are the only other baseball team — and he thinks he'd have a hard time convincing a U.S. team to hire him, a Canadian, if an American is available to do the job.

"I've often said that I have the best job in baseball, so I'm not sure that I want to move on. I'm very connected to the players, I travel with the team when I want to, the club pays me all year long, and I have plenty of time off." Ian has interests outside baseball as well. He has invested in racehorses (six horses in the past four years) and several restaurants. "I've had meetings about other projects, including a golf course. I'll listen to just about anything that comes along. It doesn't hurt to listen." The team is aware of his outside interests: "I prefer to let them know that there are no conflicts.

"The team's president took us aside and said, 'You're obviously baseball fans. Why don't you work for us?' In three seconds we said, '*Yes!!!*'"

"There are times when I say that I'd be crazy to do this until I'm fifty, and there are other times I think I'd be crazy to leave. Still, it's tough to have girlfriends on this kind of schedule, and it would be harder still with a family. But no matter what happens, I don't see myself in a traditional job at a desk with a suit and a secretary or any of that sort of stuff."

How to Become a Bat or Ball Boy

Ian supervises a staff that cares for the visiting team, including one bat boy and one ball boy, whom he hires.

When asked about what makes a good candidate for either job, Ian quotes an old clubhouse adage: "What you see here and what you hear here: Let it stay here when you leave here."

"Things that happen in the clubhouse are private and should be kept that way. If you want to be a bat or ball boy because you're out to get autographs, you're looking in the wrong place. The players get hounded by the fans; they don't need to get hounded by the people working for the team.

"I've hired kids in three different ways. First, there are children of friends. Second, there are people whom I have seen at work who have made a good impression. I hired my parents' paper carrier, for example, because he seemed to be a good worker. Most candidates apply to our baseball operations office by sending a letter. They're usually interested in the game, know a lot about the team, and can show that they're willing to work hard, keep quiet, and be professional. The operations office usually screens the candidates and sends the best ones down to me. I make the final decision."

Being a bat or ball boy is not all glamour. Certainly, it's fun to be out on the field or in the dugouts with the players during the game. But before the game, the job entails helping out in the clubhouse, keeping things neat, picking up laundry, and running errands. During batting practice, you have to keep track of every bat, every ball — every piece of equipment. During the game, the bat boy is responsible for putting the hitters' warm-up equipment in the on-deck circle every other half-inning, picking up the hitter's bat and helmet, and keeping equipment on the bench organized. Meanwhile, the ball boy, down the outfield line, has to throw with the visiting team's outfielder between innings and is responsible for fielding and collecting any foul balls that come his way. Also, when a pitching change is made, he must bring the reliever's jacket into the dugout. And after the game, it's back to the clubhouse to help out with the meal, run more errands, and pick up after the players.

"I have a small staff. It's just me, my assistant, two other attendants, one bat boy, and one ball boy. We all work together and do whatever needs to be done."

Ian's ADVICE

"One way to get a job in baseball is to be in the right place at the right time. There's a way to make yourself visible while staying low-key and not getting in anyone's way."

The best way to get started is to work as an equipment manager for your school's team. "That looks good on a resume. It shows that you understand what needs to be done, that you are willing and able to do the work. I started doing this job when I was twenty-one, which a lot of people thought was too young. But management liked the way I handled myself; I don't think I am very different today."

As for college: "The more schooling you have, the better off you are going to be in the long run. I recommend college. I went to the University of Toronto, mainly to please my parents. It wasn't right for me, though, so I left — and college is not essential for a clubhouse manager or an equipment manager. Guys who work in this part of the organization don't usually rise to top management positions in the front office. But that doesn't mean it can't happen."

Don't rule out the minor leagues. "You might work in the clubhouse or in the concession booth selling food or souvenirs. This is one way to meet people who are on their way up. And it's a good way to learn about baseball."

Ian cautions anyone who thinks of minor league ball as just a stepping-stone, however. "It's very tough to get a major league job. There are only twenty-six visiting clubhouse managers, and there are lots of minor league guys waiting to move up."

What if you're a woman? Ian is doubtful about a woman's chances of getting this particular job. "In Europe, a naked body is a naked body — there's nothing shocking about it. But here in North America, a lot of players would be uncomfortable if the person in charge of the clubhouse were female. Yes, there are female reporters in the clubhouse, and some female trainers in the minor leagues. Still, I'm not sure that we'll ever see a female clubhouse manager, at least not in the major leagues." ■

Video Producer
CHARLES STEINBERG

Charles Steinberg is in charge of Orioles Productions and all in-stadium entertainment. He is also a dentist.

"Growing up, I was never an especially strong player. I became a baseball fan during the celebration of the 1966 World Championship, when the Orioles won four straight in Baltimore. I remember my mother drove me and my sister to the celebration. It was a very big deal, people shouting, honking car horns — everybody in Baltimore was so excited. I got two autographs that night. Starting in 1967, I became a rabid fan. I knew the name of every player on the Orioles, every player's uniform number, endless statistics. . . . It just poured in. I was a typical nine-year-old baseball nut. I remember my sister took me to the library and told the librarian that I adored any book about baseball. It continued as a passionate hobby through elementary school and junior high."

In high school, Charles became the JV baseball team's statistician. People took him seriously. "When I said that I was going to take off from JV baseball practice to go to the Orioles' opening day — I had been to every one since fourth grade — someone said, 'Wow, you mean you do stats for the Orioles, too?'"

Charles attended the Gilman School, a private high school in Baltimore. "In the last month of senior year, the school ran what they called the Encounter Program. The school set you up anywhere you wanted, to do volunteer work for a month. We were told to choose something that

we wanted to do when we finished school or else something that we'd never have the chance to do again. At first I thought I should be practical. I planned to be a pediatric dentist. My father was an orthodontist, and I had helped around his office for years. Working with a pediatric dentist would be the smart thing to do, I thought. Then a classmate told me that someone from the school had done an Encounter with the Orioles. Practicality went out the window. I figured, I'll never have a chance to do this again. Both my classmate and I called up Jack Dunn, a vice president of the Orioles, whose name I knew because his family used to own the Orioles in the 1920s, when it was a minor league team (I really knew my Orioles history). He arranged a meeting with Bob Brown, the Orioles public relations director.

Before the meeting, Charles had his doubts, because he thought that public relations was nothing more than dealing with complaints from public. He soon saw otherwise. "I was overwhelmed. The PR department is the information center of the entire team. Bob handed us both a media guide — and told us to memorize the entire book before the first day (he was joking). But browsing through that media guide, with all of those facts and statistics, gave me a healthy dose of what went on behind the scenes."

Charles's first day with the Orioles was May 6. "It was two days before a big Brooks Robinson promotion day. We were going to give out thousands of orange-colored Orioles jerseys, each with Brooks's number, five, on it. I helped move boxes of those jerseys to each of the gates. I never thought much about how this kind of work was done — things don't just happen: people take care of the details. And now, at least for a short time, I was one of those people. As I showed that I could handle the more mundane tasks competently, my assignments became more complicated. I pasted articles in the official Orioles scrapbook. I stamped players' names on slides that we sent to the television stations. While I was working, I could hear the public relations director talking to a new player, Reggie Jackson, getting information for a short bio."

When the month was over, the internship was over. What Charles didn't know was that his enthusiasm, even for the menial tasks, was something special. The Orioles management remembered him, and when ABC came to cover a game, Charles was hired to help out. "I got to sit on the field by the third base cameraman. I had to wear a towel when we were in commercial break. The third base umpire looked at me. If I had a towel on, then we were in the commercial break. If the towel was off, they could resume play." Another day, he was hired to straighten out a storeroom. Fascinated by the "neat stuff" in the storeroom, Charles thoroughly enjoyed himself. "I just started volunteering to help out, to do whatever needed to be done. My mom let me use her car to get to and from the stadium. I'd come into the office and say, 'I'm here, if anyone needs me.'"

That summer, Charles worked as a lifeguard at a day camp — and showed up at the stadium on game nights to help out. "I knew that I was going to college for dentistry, at the University of Maryland, starting in the fall. Baseball was something fun to do during the summer before college. I had no reason to believe that I would have anything more to do with the Orioles once the summer was over."

In the fall, he went away to school, in College Park, Maryland. When he came home between semesters, he visited Bob Brown at the Orioles office. Bob asked him about his plans for the following summer. "He told me he'd like me to work with them every day. I worked Opening Day. I came back in mid-May, while I was taking the pre-dental courses. I was amazed at what he gave me to do. First he found me a desk — my own desk at Memorial Stadium! Then he plunked down thirteen large envelopes and said, 'These are Earl Weaver's statistics,' and told me to compile them. Here he was, handing me official information that was vital to the team's strategies — a sheet for every opposing pitcher in the league, with a list of each player on our team, giving base hits, doubles, triples, RBIs, walks, and strikeouts, for both lifetime and

"I just started volunteering to help out, to do whatever needed to be done."

that year. These were the stats that Weaver used to determine the lineups and choose pinch-hitters. Now I wasn't just *helping out* the PR department; I was actually doing the work. Since Bob knew that I was good with math and statistics, he started asking me to compile information for the game notes — the information that we provide to the writers and broadcasters each day, the information that they use to write and talk about the Orioles. I was honored. I didn't find the work difficult, but everything had to be perfect, and that was a challenge. The research was fun. We drew 100,000 fans in a three-game home stand — was that the best attended series in our history? We won twelve games in a row — was that the best in the team's history? I learned to anticipate the questions that the media would ask."

As Charles headed into his junior year, he started to hear a familiar refrain from associates, friends, and family: "So, now that you're starting on the toughest part of college, I guess you'll have to leave the Orioles." Charles would not respond. Instead, he said to himself, "Well, why should I leave, exactly?" Unable to come up with a good reason, he continued working with the team.

The 1979 season was a spectacular one for the Orioles. They came from behind and sustained a level of excellence all year long. "With a pennant-style season comes heightened interest in your team. Our PR department was feeling the pressure. *Sports Illustrated* would come in and do a week-long story. There were countless phone calls. Bob Brown got very busy, so he started to hand me some of his more time-consuming tasks. That's when I started writing on the scoreboard. While the game was in progress, I wrote simple notes on the two-line scoreboard display, listing Orioles batting leaders, league leaders, that sort of thing. If Ken Singleton was leading the league, I'd check to see if he was also leading the majors, and write the piece. Bob Brown still wrote the really clever stuff, but I did my best. After the game, I started going down to the clubhouse to get quotes for writers who were too busy filing post-game stories to get down there themselves. By the time the World Series began, we were swamped. I was basically writing the scoreboard myself, and I learned to do it with some drama. During the series, I had a big announcement that I knew the crowd would love. When the moment was just right, I wrote: 'Congratulations to Orioles Manager Earl Weaver,' named today as the *Sporting News* Major League Manager of the Year.' The place went wild, in part because of the timing. With tens of thousands of people in the stadium, baseball is theater — it's entertainment."

With college now over, Charles headed for dental school. "People said, 'Of course *now* you'll have to quit working for the Orioles.' I knew dental school was going to be demanding, but I wasn't going to leave baseball prematurely. I figured I would stay with baseball until it became a problem. My work load was similar: during the game, it was scoreboard work, and before and after, I did notes and quotes. During the game, I was counting pitches, how many balls, strikes, and typing a play-by-play report, in addition to scoring the game on a scorecard. I was having a great time."

The University of Maryland's Dental School is located in downtown Baltimore, not far from the stadium. The program was thoroughly demanding, so Charles reduced his Orioles workload during the school year. In May, when the school year ended, and baseball's seasonal demands increased, Charles simply spent more time working with the Orioles. He was needed; the interest in Orioles baseball was at an all-time high.

By his second year of dental school, Charles still didn't believe that the work with the Orioles was anything more than fun. Then a fellow student discovered an article in the *Journal of the American Dental Association* that mentioned the effect of mouth appliances on athletic performance. Charles began to wonder whether there was any connection between baseball and dentistry. He attended a symposium at University of Michigan for dentists; he was the only student in attendance, but he wanted to know as much as he

Mouth Appliance:
An object attached to the mouth, usually for a medical or training purpose.

Corporate Marketing Communications Tape:
Marketing communications is another way of saying promotion, or public relations. This type of videotape is used to educate outsiders about a corporation. In Charles's case, he produces tapes about the Orioles — describing its activities and explaining why the team needs financial support from companies based in Baltimore.

could about the emerging field of sports dentistry. The symposium included dentists from some university football teams. He participated in an informal research project, but the results were inconclusive.

"My work with the Orioles continued, but as time went on, there was more of it. I had always been interested in the way that music can punctuate the drama of a situation, and I started integrating music into my scoreboard work. By now, dental school faculty members were telling me that I'd have to drop out of dental school or leave the Orioles, that my junior year at dental school was going to be too demanding to handle both successfully. That summer, I was working in a clinic, starting to treat patients, and I couldn't slow down the patient care in order to do the baseball work. Finally, Bob Brown came to me and said that I'd probably have to make a decision. He needed me, and I was just not there enough to get the work done. I said, 'Let's look ahead. Next May, I graduate from dental school, and for most of the next summer, I will not be able to practice dentistry because I'll be waiting for my license. If we can weather this season, then when I graduate, I can be here day and night.' To be honest, neither one of us really knew where the whole relationship was heading, but he liked me, and the whole experience had been wonderful for me. So I continued."

Despite the demands of dental school, Charles managed to devote a lot of time to the Orioles. He traveled with the team through the World Series. "We stayed in fancy hotels. The team's star, Eddie Murray, had a room right across the hall from me. We went out to lunch one day — I felt like I was walking on air. The whole nation was focused on what our team was doing, and here I was, having lunch with the star player. This was far beyond what I thought I would do in baseball."

When Charles began his private practice, he shared an office with several other dentists. He worked five days a week with the Orioles and saw patients in the evenings and on Saturdays. As the practice grew, he planned to cut back from five to four to three days a week with the Orioles.

In late December, Bob Brown told Charles that the Orioles would be getting a new Diamondvision screen. He asked Charles to take charge of the project. Within a short time, Charles realized that Diamondvision required a working knowledge of video production. Charles knew nothing whatsoever about video, but he was smart enough to realize that he had two options: he could hire a video technician who would be assisted by a PR person, or he could hire a baseball PR person and teach them video production. He chose the latter, hired a staff, and quickly realized that video production is extraordinarily time-consuming. "I was now working one afternoon in another dentist's office and teaching one day a week at the dental school. I cut down on the dental work to make time to work with the new scoreboard. The board was installed on March 19, less than a month before the start of the season. "I basically gave the staff a list of images I wanted to create. We started producing small features — a video montage of Rick Dempsey, our gutsy catcher, accompanied by the Pat Benatar song 'Hit Me with Your Best Shot,' for example. We'd show a sequence from a given season, play a song that was popular at the time, and challenge fans to guess the year. So here I was, a video producer with no video background at all. And I really started to enjoy the work."

The board proved to be a hit with the fans. Since the Orioles were now in the video production business — they had purchased cameras, a switcher, lights, and other equipment to support Diamondvision — Charles and his group were asked to produce a ten-minute marketing tape to encourage area businesses to become involved with the Orioles. "Suddenly, I was writing a corporate mar-

keting communications tape — and learning more than ever. The tape was extremely well received. Midway through the next season, Rick Dempsey, who was already a folk hero in Baltimore, went into a recording studio and recorded five rock songs with a band. He gave them to me, hoping that I'd play them in the ballpark. I was stunned by the potential that these songs had — they could really get the crowd going. One of them, 'Old Time Rock and Roll,' was a natural for a music video. Imagine the excitement of the fans if they saw the players recording the song! We rented instruments and shot some of the athletes playing — they weren't really playing, but it really was Rick singing. We used that video in late June 1986, and it brought the house down! It added a whole new dimension to ballpark entertainment."

After a series of video successes, Charles started producing annual team highlights tapes to sell to fans. He accepted a new title: game communications coordinator, and eventually took charge of all ballpark entertainment, including music, public address, scoreboard, Diamondvision, presentation of field ceremonies, and home video. Charles is having the time of his life.

"My part-time dentistry practice is now limited to Saturdays and evenings. If a patient needs me, other dentists cover for me. My practice is as full as I allow it to be, and I'm not allowing it to grow. I'm also the club's dentist, so my patients include the Orioles players, their families, and the visiting players. Dentistry is still an important part of my life. But I never arbitrarily made the decision between baseball and dentistry. As I sit back, I would never have believed that any of this would happen. I have no special qualities or abilities. I just worked my tail off, which is easy to do when you love something as much as I love baseball. I didn't know anybody in baseball — I just found myself in a lucky situation, did the best job I knew how to do, and stuck with it for as long as I possibly could."

How a Scoreboard Works

"We have two scoreboards. One is a traditional black-and-white board that we use to show information about the game in progress. The other is called Diamondvision; it's a color video scoreboard."

About ten people are required to operate the Diamondvision system. One person operates a still-frame storage system, which shows still pictures that are stored electronically on a large computer disk. The still store is used to display a picture of the player's face, for example. The bottom half of the video picture is usually text, such as the player's name and some statistics. This information is supplied by another computer called the character generator. Letters typed on a keyboard appear on the screen. The images from the still store and the character generator are combined in a kind of split screen by yet another machine called the video switcher.

The switcher is the center of the entire system. With its many buttons, it is used to select any video input, including cameras, videotape playback, slow-motion video, character generator, or still store. These images can be made more interesting with special video effects that are also included with the switcher's circuitry. Above the switcher are eighteen monitors showing all of the video options. The person who operates the switcher also makes the selections; the job of the traditional television director is usually done by the switcher, or on occasion by the producer.

Two cameras cover the action — one just behind home plate, to give the entire stadium the best possible view of the action, and another in the upper deck, for fan close-ups and other shots. The switcher also has access to the images from the cameras used by the local broadcaster — five cameras strategically positioned above first and third base, above home plate, and down in the dugout areas.

"The video side is only part of the story. We also have someone watching out-of-town games so we can show updates to fans. We use the Diamondvision computer as a second graphics device to show lineups and scores of all the games in the league. A production assistant keeps score, runs and gets sodas, and makes sure that the camerapeople get water on hot days. We also have an audio technician — a sound engineer — who plays music and the sound from videotapes. We have a library of traditional music for the ballpark, but we also have over a hundred speciality songs. If a cat runs out on the field, we have music for that. When the Orioles make a pitching change, when there's a rain delay, when we win or lose or go into extra innings, we have music for everything. We even have music to play if there's a power outage — but we're not sure how we would play it if we have no power for the sound system.

"So far, we've talked about eight people: the still store operator, the character generator operator, the switcher, the Diamondvision graphics operator, two camera operators, the production assistant, and the audio technician. We also have an engineer, the nuts-and-bolts person who can fix anything that breaks. The person in charge — that's my role — is the producer, who is always coming up with ideas to make the whole ballpark experience more fun and more enjoyable."

The scoreboard at the new Memorial Stadium at Camden Yards.

Charles's ADVICE

In order to succeed in baseball, or in almost any career, you need four qualities. First, you must have integrity — you must care about what you do. Second, you should be bright, which doesn't necessarily mean being good in school — it means that you are paying attention. Third, you have to be willing to work hard. Fourth, you have to work well with other people. If you have those four qualities, you are far ahead of most workers. It really is that simple.

"As you try to figure out what you want to do with your life, think about what makes you really happy. Close your eyes and picture yourself doing something that you love to do. Now make the decision that you can aim for that. Don't limit your dreams by what seems practical at the moment. Whenever somebody says, 'That career is too competitive,' or 'You won't make money in that career,' listen to what they have to say, but do what your heart tells you.

"I'm looking for people with positive attitudes who believe that they can be who they want to be — it's always easier for me to hire someone who believes that anything is possible. I can't promise everyone that their dreams will come true, but dreams sure won't come true if you stop dreaming."

Charles feels that a college education is vitally important. "I don't care how much you know about baseball — I won't hire anyone in video production without a college degree. I want somebody with a well-rounded formal education, who can write, spell, and use English correctly."

To learn more about video and scoreboards, contact the director of scoreboard or video operations at your local team. You can find the person's name in the team's yearbook or media guide.

The best way to get started is with an internship. Encourage your high school to arrange internships. And college internships are essential. "Given the choice of two bright, hard-working candidates with college educations, I will always choose the one who has done one or more internships. Without the internships, all I know is that the candidate managed to get through school. But the one who has gone through several internships has already developed a professional reputation; there are other employers I can call and talk to. Baseball has become a competitive business; you must intern, and I prefer to see people who have begun interning in high school." ∎

Business Operations Executive
DENNIS LEHMAN

Dennis Lehman is the senior vice president of business operations for the Cleveland Indians.

On a game day, I usually get to the stadium at 8:00 A.M. I sit down at my desk and read the newspaper, scanning for information about the city, about activities that we might become involved in, and about street closures and construction traffic that may affect the fans. I also read the baseball news and the columnists, to see what people are saying about the team and our players."

By about nine, Dennis moves from one department to another, checking on every aspect of the Indians operation. "I spend a lot of time in ticket operations, discussing sales. If we know the advance sale, we can estimate the number of ticket sellers, concession people, ushers, parking attendants, and security guards that we'll need for the game. The police also need to know the size of the crowd we're expecting, so they can make their plans for directing traffic. We sweep all of the available information — the advance sale, the phone activity on that day, the excitement of last night's game, the drawing power of the visiting team — there are a lot of factors. A computer gives us some of the information, but we also base the decision on gut feelings. And then of course, the final factor is weather — that's a big determining factor of how many people will come to the game."

By mid-morning, Dennis settles into meetings and planning sessions on longer-term projects. "We're planning a new downtown baseball park, and we're at the stage now where we're looking at a lot of numbers: how much it would cost, for example, to build not only a stadium but an arena for the Cavaliers next door. Our vice president of marketing and I are taking charge of the ballpark." Other long-term projects may be less magnificent — a new computerized accounting system, a change in the menu at the concession stands, employee policies and procedures. And there's a tremendous amount of mail to read and answer every day.

After lunch out with other Cleveland executives, Dennis usually returns to a pile of phone messages. "I try to return all of my calls every afternoon. I negotiate the broadcast rights agreements, and I see our team as a kind of partner in these broadcast arrangements, so we usually help out with finding sponsors and keeping them interested in the game. I'm often on the phone with the general manager at WWWE radio (they do all of our radio coverage, plus twenty spring training games), and the television rights holders, WUAB (they do sixty games each year) and SportsChannel Ohio (they do forty-five). In addition, ESPN covers some of the games, and they usually give us a week or two's notice when they're coming to town. If they're coming, I handle the basic arrangements. It's the same with CBS, which broadcasts Major League Baseball nationally."

"Essentially, I'm concerned about getting people into the ballpark — as many people as possible."

Dennis also spends some time each day with the Indians' marketing department. "Essentially, I'm concerned with getting people into the ballpark — as many people as possible. The marketing department develops promotions — giveaways, special arrangements with local car dealers, ideas that help to fill the seats — and I approve them. Then I usually take a walk around the stadium and check to be sure that it's clean, that the field looks good, that any problems have been solved. I usually stop by the ticket office to see how sales are going for that day's games.

Lingo

Broadcast Rights Agreement:
Every baseball team owns the right to broadcast its own games. This right is usually sold to area radio and television stations and to regional cable networks. The negotiated contract includes the amount of money that will be paid to the team, the number of games that can be broadcast, the number of seasons that the agreement runs, and other business details.

Sponsors:
Another word for advertisers who pay money to the broadcaster or cable network so that their commercials are seen or heard within specific programs.

ESPN:
A cable television network specializing in sports programming.

Bottom Line:
When you subtract the amount of money that you've taken in (income) from the amount of money you've spent (expenses), the result appears at the bottom of the budget ledger page. If the bottom line is a positive number, then you've made money. If it's a negative number, you've lost money.

"Sometimes I stop by to see Hank Peters, the club's president. We talk about the team, the outcome of yesterday's game, plans, other teams and what they're up to. We also discuss player contracts and how they affect our bottom line — we have several free agents in the current club — we signed them last winter for what we thought were reasonable amounts of money. They were one-year contracts, but now the players want extensions, longer contracts. We have to figure out whether these players are worth the money. Do these players help the club offensively, defensively, with pitching? Do they bring people to the stadium? Cleveland is not a large market like New York or Los Angeles; we deal with more modest budgets. We try not to dip into the free agent market; we'd much rather develop our talent from within the organization. Hank Peters is in charge of player development; he runs the club itself, the scouting, the major and minor league organization."

Later in the afternoon, Dennis makes certain that the stadium and the entire support operation are ready to handle the crowd. By about five or six, everything is set. This is Dennis's quiet time in the office, to return just a few more phone calls, work at the computer, and if time permits, answer more letters.

All major league stadiums have a dining room for working press and team executives. "I usually eat with Hank Peters and watch a few innings with him. Then I walk around the stadium to make sure everything is going all right. I usually stop off a few times to visit with friends in the stands. Sometimes my wife and children come to the games, so I sit and watch an inning or two with them. I carry a portable phone and keep a diary with me, to make notes on what needs to be done for the next day. I also watch the weather. In our location weather can change very quickly; sometimes we get a lot of rain."

A half hour after the game is over, he goes home. It's a long day, but Dennis, like many baseball professionals, knows that this job is a childhood dream come true.

"Growing up in Philadelphia, I'd go to lots of major league games at Connie Mack Stadium with my dad. I fantasized that we would be teammates — he'd play in the infield, and I'd be in the outfield. I dreamed that we were both Phillies stars. I always followed the Phillies and the National League. I was very loyal; I didn't pay a lot of attention to the other clubs. I also played Little League ball. I was a second baseman, and I played some left field. I had decent speed but not much power. I never got very far with it. I also played basketball and golf with my buddies a few days a week. On weekends, I would go with my dad to the hospital — he was an obstetrician. As he made his rounds through the maternity ward, he'd introduce me to his patients. It was very high tech; I think I was more interested in medicine than baseball.

"I was always working when I was a kid; I had a paper route, and I was a caddy. My school required tuition, and my parents taught me responsibility by having me pay the bills for my own schooling."

It was Dennis's work as a caddy that prompted his move into professional sports. "One of the golfers, who was also a neighbor of mine, sold tickets for the Phillies, and I used to pester him about getting a job with the team. This went on for a few summers, but nothing came of it. I wasn't sure what I wanted to do, but I knew I was looking for something different. Being a caddy was hard work. Then he called to tell me that Bill Giles was moving up from Houston to take over the Phillies and that he was going to make a lot of changes. They needed runners to bring food and drinks to the working press. My neighbor arranged an interview with Tony Siegel, who had worked with Bill in Houston and was now the director of operations. I think he liked me because I was willing to work in the office, not just at the games. Boy, it was a big thrill to walk into an office at Connie Mack Stadium and leave knowing that I was going to work for the Phillies!"

A short time later, Larry Shenk, head of public relations for the Phillies, called to ask Dennis to work with him on preparations for

"I fantasized that my dad and I would be teammates. I dreamed that we were both Phillies stars."

the move into the new stadium. "I started a week later, helping his secretary/assistant perform general public relations functions like making copies of game notes, typing letters, doing whatever had to be done."

When the season began, Dennis became one of two press box runners. "We wore these white outfits with the new Phillies *P* logo. We looked like Good Humor men. It was my first experience with the media; I got them sandwiches and soft drinks and came to know them personally. I became a part of the team family, got to know John Quinn, the general manager, and many of the players and coaches. That was the beginning of a long relationship."

Dennis stayed with the Phillies for eighteen years.

"I remember a conversation with Bill Giles my first year. He asked me if I wanted to leave college to work full-time in their public relations department. I thought this was nice, but I also thought it might be shortsighted on my part to accept the offer. Instead, I worked when I could during the school year and worked summers until I was out of school. But I had my own desk in the public relations department, and I was there when we moved into the new stadium. It was a big kick.

"When the scoreboard operator left, I talked Bill and Larry into letting me operate it, and I did that for many years. I was a rah-rah type in high school, and that part of my personality really took hold. We had these giant clapping hands on the scoreboard, and we developed all sorts of crazy stuff. Between my scoreboard and Dan Baker, the P.A. announcer, we were able to control the crowd. That was a lot of fun."

Larry taught Dennis how to write press releases. Dennis also learned to answer the mail. He filed live radio reports, recaps of each game, with a local Philadelphia radio station. This led to work with the advertising agencies that sponsored Phillies broadcasts. Eventually, Dennis became the director of the Phillies radio network. A short time later, he became the club's marketing director, and among his many responsibilities was the sale of stadium advertising space ("those big signs in the outfield or on the scoreboard — we charge up to $250,000 a year to advertise on them"). Dennis was also responsible for the Phillies' contract with PRISM, a regional cable sports network, and he cleverly retained the right to sell advertising in the broadcasts. In short, Dennis seemed to know, almost by instinct, how to turn a good business proposition into one that was even more profitable.

"I was really very happy with the Phillies, but one day, Bill Giles and the Phillies executive VP, Dave Montgomery, came into my office with a surprise. They told me that Hank Peters, who had just left Baltimore for Cleveland, was interested in having me work in the Indians organization. I assumed that I was going to be offered the VP of marketing job, a good step up for me. I had a few conversations by phone with Hank, and then my wife and I decided to visit Cleveland. That's when I realized that the job wasn't just marketing — it was running the entire business operation! I think he had been talking to a lot of people about me. I'm pretty enthusiastic, I handle people pretty well, and I certainly saw the opportunity. I asked for the job, and he gave it to me. The people at the Phillies weren't anxious to see me go, but everyone understood that this was a very exciting opportunity for me. There really wasn't much more for me to do in Philadelphia; the time was right to move on.

"I'm still learning, but there isn't a whole lot that I do day-to-day that I haven't done before. But I'm still fresh, and I certainly understand that what worked in Philadelphia may not necessarily work here in Cleveland. Also, we're a smaller organization; we had more than eighty people in the Phillies front office, but here, there are less than fifty. Still, I was able to hire most of my own staff, and it's gratifying to see people grow. All in all, I'm having a very good time."

"I understand that what worked in Philadelphia may not necessarily work here in Cleveland."

Dennis's ADVICE

"I think you've got to be really well rounded. If you're serious about sports management, you've got to be able to absorb and retain a lot of information. One way to practice is to read a lot. Professional baseball involves a lot of research — player stats, for example, or attendance figures and how they affect the bottom line. Learning where to go for information, how to use a library, and how to read quickly to get good in-depth information are all important. You'd be surprised at how much the skills you develop by reading novels and studying for school help when you're working in management.

"Whether you're thinking about playing the game or working in the front office, you have to like the sport. That means playing a lot — it's more than muscle training; it's mental training, too. Even if you're not the best player, the training will help you develop discipline, and it will certainly help you to understand the game. And if you manage or coach a Little League or an amateur team, you will learn a great deal about leadership.

"I always thought of college as an opportunity to learn as much as possible about as many different topics as possible. The subject I learned the most about, however, was myself and what makes me tick. I also learned that struggling to identify a career too early is probably not a good idea — if it comes naturally, fine, but don't force it. If you're interested in history or in English, stay with it; it won't hurt you to do the course work. A sports management degree is fine but not essential.

"Either way, you're going to need experience — if you are near any professional franchise, get involved in a very low-level job. I think the best opportunities are at the minor league level, where you'll have a chance to learn about the field, concessions, tickets, and advertising sales. Minor leagues give you a concentrated education — because there's a small staff, everyone does everything. When I'm reading a resume, I look for experience, some time learning on the job. I want to see someone who has been out there hustling — someone who's sold a bit or who's had some experience in a fast food restaurant — and has as much experience working with people as possible. But most of all, I want to see that determination, that desire, and that look in your eyes that tells me that you can do the job better than anyone else." ∎

Major League Pitcher
STEVE FREY

I grew up in Southhampton, about an hour's drive north of Philadelphia. There is a real community here. I was involved in the Southhampton Sports Club from the time I was about seven until I was eighteen. I went from T-ball to Babe Ruth League. I played basketball; I played football. I was a sports fanatic. When I wasn't playing sports or going to school, I was watching sports on TV. I was always a pitcher when I played baseball, but I was a good enough athlete that I could hit, too. I sometimes played the outfield; in high school and even in college, a lot of pitchers also played in the outfield."

Steve's interest in sports came from his family. "My father played softball, and when he got older, he became an umpire in the Southhampton Sports Club. My mother was the first woman president of the Sports Club. My brother played baseball at Bucks County Community College, and he was a big inspiration for me. He's eleven years older than me, and he was one of the best pitchers in the area. I used to love to watch him pitch. He played semi-pro ball in the PennDel League. He was a right-handed pitcher, a consistent all-star. He was scouted by the big leagues, but it didn't work out for him. I was eight years old at the

Steve Frey has been a relief pitcher with the Montreal Expos.

time, and I remember thinking maybe someday I could pitch at his caliber."

As a teenager, Steve's time was occupied mostly with sports. "There was sports and school; I wasn't much interested in girls at that age. But I realized that I was not going to be big physically, and if I was going to pursue a sport, it would have to be baseball. I felt that baseball was what I did best, but like any other kid, playing major league ball was just a dream. I had no idea whether I could take the next steps or not. But when I turned fifteen, I pitched in a championship game, and I had fifteen strikeouts. I thought maybe that was a sign. I was also starting to get some press in the local newspapers. My coach said I'd be a future star in the area; he thought I would have a good high school career."

The coach was right. Steve's varsity pitching record was 17–4. "I was disappointed that I wasn't picked up in the major league June draft, when the best high school players are picked up. I had been seeing scouts at our games all through my junior and senior years, always scribbling something into their notepads. Southeastern Pennsylvania is known as a very competitive baseball area, so the scouts are always visiting schools there, looking at kids that they've heard about. When I wasn't drafted, I figured it was because of my size. But I never let that bother me, because there was nothing I could do about it."

After a game in the PennDel League, Steve was taking off his spikes when he was approached by a scout for one of the American League teams. "He said, 'Steve, we think you're a pretty good pitcher, and we'd like you to sign on with us.' By now I knew all about signing bonuses because I'd been reading about them in the newspapers. I asked him, 'What kind of money are we talking about here?' and he told me, 'Well, we are going to give you six hundred dollars a month, and we're ready to send you to rookie league in Butte, Montana.' I asked, 'Is there a signing bonus involved here?' He said no, and I turned the offer down. I had my mind set on going to Bucks County Community College to further my education and to continue to play ball. It just didn't feel right to me."

Steve's confidence soared. "I knew that if one scout had asked me to sign, then other people were probably interested as well. I knew I was going to get a chance to go away, at least to a minor league team. And then I started to hear stories about guys who went away for two weeks only to be released. I figured, if they got their shot, I was going to get mine as well. I knew I was a good pitcher. There was no insecurity on my part. I continued playing summer ball and working out with guys who kept telling me I had what it took. To make sure I would have the chance, they tutored me all summer long. With their help, I became even more sure of myself."

Steve continued to go to tryouts. A coach arranged for a tryout for the Pan Am Games. Five hundred kids showed up, and Steve wondered how anyone would get a fair shake. He didn't get a callback. He went to another tryout for the Dodgers, and again, there were too many people. Still, he retained his confidence. He knew that scouts were coming to watch him pitch, scouts who were going to his games mainly to judge his individual performance.

Now a student at Bucks County Community College, Steve continued pitching with the Jenkintown Quakers in the PennDel League. An area scout for the Yankees convinced a more senior scout to come to see Steve pitch. "I remember he left after the fourth inning. I thought, Oh, no! What's going on? My local scout stayed back and told me that the senior scout liked what he saw. I couldn't understand what the guy saw, because I didn't pitch real well that day. The scout told me he was looking for how quickly I warmed up (which would tell him whether I'd be a starter or a reliever). Being left-

Major League Pitcher

> "Here I am standing on this perfect pitcher's mound in the middle of Yankee Stadium. It's just great — my blood is flowing, and my arm is feeling good. I pitched nine out of ten strikes."

handed obviously helped. He looked at my mechanics, realizing that the organization would build on what I already knew."

Steve was invited to a tryout at Yankee Stadium. "I had pitched the day before, but I always had a rubber arm — I could throw every day. When I got there, they asked me to throw ten pitches. I went up to the mound — and suddenly, my dream just got a whole lot bigger! Here I am standing on this perfect pitcher's mound in the middle of Yankee Stadium. It's just great — my blood is flowing, and my arm is feeling good. They asked me if I'd pitched recently, and I told them I had pitched seven innings yesterday. Then I pitched nine out of ten strikes. I felt good, really good, about how I got out there and threw. A week later I was drafted."

To this day, Steve remembers every detail about where he was when he got the call. "The scout said, 'Congratulations, you've just been drafted by the New York Yankees.' I was scheduled to become a reliever for the Oneonta Yankees, who played in the Class A New York–Penn League. And I received a signing bonus."

Oneonta, New York, is only five hours north of Steve's home in Bucks County, Pennsylvania. When he arrived, he was a little surprised. "I looked out on the field and I got my first taste of reality. There were twenty pitchers, plus thirty more players. I wasn't intimidated, but all of the pitchers were real big. At five-nine, I was one of the smallest players on the team. With all of those pitchers, I was thinking, I'm never going to pitch. The season is only three months long, from late June until late August. I'm just going to get a few innings here. Then I started seeing the business of baseball. All of a sudden, guys are being released, sent down to rookie ball. Other guys are getting sent up to AA, and we become a regular size team. All of this happened after only a few weeks. Most important of all, I was having *fun*. I was having a great season. And I said to myself, I'm going to get to the big leagues. My dream is so alive right now! I was the number-one stopper in the bull pen. When the season was over, the local newspaper awarded me Most Valuable Player. It was just a great feeling. Now my sights were set on the big leagues, but I knew I wasn't going to go from Class A to the majors. I was going to have to take gradual steps."

In January, Steve was assigned to the Fort Lauderdale Yankees, a high-A league team that played a full 140-game season. "It was a nice jump. I didn't have to play in the South Atlantic League, like many players did. And I liked Florida — it was warm; I liked the sun, and I like to pitch in warm weather. I stayed in Florida through spring training and through the season."

Steve had another good season. He was invited to instructional league, where the most promising minor leaguers play after the regular season. During the winter, he became engaged. "My fiancee was attending nursing school, I was at the Class A level, and we didn't know what our future was going to be like. We weren't going to get any richer or any poorer if we got married. I got back from instructional league on November 15, came home, got married, and got a job working in a shipping department to earn money through the off-season."

That winter, Steve set a goal for himself: he wanted to reach the big leagues by his fifth year. Based on his progress, he was confident that this was possible. During spring training, he worked out with the AA team, the Albany-Colonie (New York) Yankees. On the very last day of spring training, he got bumped by what players call the domino effect — players from the major league team and AAA being dropped down a level, causing the AA team to drop a player as well. "I knew I didn't belong back in Class A, but I went down there with a good attitude. I played three weeks in Class A again, proved I didn't belong, and spent the rest of the year in Albany." Steve realized how lucky he was — Albany, like Oneonta, was driving distance from home. He had another good year and began to get used to seeing fellow players get sent up and down.

He spent the off-season working as a painter. In January, he got a contract with the Columbus (Ohio) Clippers, the Yankees AAA team. He worked out at AAA camp, but again the domino effect caused him to start the season with a lower-level team. "Once again I proved I didn't belong, and halfway through the season, I made the big jump to AAA. I was starting to see a lot of players who were trying to get back up to the top. I went up there for a month, and my pitches got hit all over the place. My ERA jumped to something like 8.00. I kept asking myself, Why are these guys successful here when I'm not? My pitching coach asked me to develop a sinker. I spent the rest of the season developing the new pitch in AA, and I finished really strong. Now I had a sinker, a fastball, and a curveball, but I really didn't have a great change-up back then. I had one, but I hardly threw it. I knew that I had to develop these pitches further in order to get back up that ladder."

The following year, Steve missed most of spring training because of a minor case of tendonitis. After rehabbing and getting better, he was activated for two weeks in AA in Albany, New York, and did well. Next he moved up to Columbus, Ohio, for the rest of the season, and the team won the league championship and the International League pennant.

During the off-season, Steve worked for an electrical contractor. In December, he was put on the Yankees roster for the first time. Things were looking great. He made plans to go to big league camp. "Then one day, as I got home from work, my wife came walking out of the house, and she looked at me real funny. She said, 'You won't believe who I just got off the phone with. The general manager of the Yankees. You've just been traded to the Mets.' I knew the Yankees organization; I knew the competition I'd have to beat out in upcoming years. But now I was joining a brand-new organization I knew nothing about, and I was going from the American League to the National League. I started thinking, Who are the Mets' left-handed pitchers? I knew I wasn't going to beat out the Mets' closer, and I didn't know much about the other left-hander.

"I reported to the Mets' training camp at Port Saint Lucie, Florida. When the first cut came along, I was cut. I went down to minor league camp and had a good spring. I went to play for the Mets AAA team in Tidewater, Virginia, near Virginia Beach. I tied the team record for the most appearances — fifty-eight — and had a really good year.

"I also had a little disappointment in midseason, and I came to understand more about the business of baseball. I was in Syracuse, New York. I had just struck out seven of the eight batters I faced. I had heard the day before that one pitcher was on the DL — the disabled list. He was a mid-reliever. And the Mets traded one of the left-handers. Now there were two spots open on the Mets pitching staff. I thought, This is my big chance. Everyone figured I'd get my shot. I was pitching great; my stats were really good. But they went out and filled the roster spot with a guy with more experience. I had a little trouble understanding why they went for a guy who was released by another team instead of letting me show my talent in the big leagues."

After about a week of what Steve calls "mental adjustment," he took a good look at himself in the mirror and decided to shake it off. His team won the division but lost the championship. "My wife and I decided that, the next year, my fourth season, I would be in the big leagues. We moved to Florida, and I worked out every day until spring training. Mentally and physically, I was prepared in every way to make that club. Going into spring training, the Mets had only one left-handed reliever. Most managers like to have a middle man and a set-up man in the bull pen. I pitched well all through spring training, but again, I was cut from the roster on the first cut. I had a meeting with the Mets' manager, and he told me that my numbers were impressive but I needed more innings. He spoke with the manager of Tidewater and told him to give me lots of innings. I said to myself, I'll prove that I don't belong there.

> "I was pitching great; my stats were really good. But they went out and filled the roster spot with a guy with more experience."

expos

So I went to minor league spring training camp.

"I was pitching against the Indianapolis Indians, the AAA affiliate of the Montreal Expos. It was not one of my best games. As I'm walking into the clubhouse, the Mets VP of baseball operations comes up and puts his arm around me (I know something's up). He said, 'Steve, can I talk to you for a moment?' My wife was watching the whole thing. She knew, without hearing the words, that I was traded.

"My mind is spinning. I'm thinking, Where am I going this time? Montreal. Well, that's good. I'm to report to Expos spring training for the next four days. I met the Expos' operational director for minor leagues. He told me he was glad to have me. And then I finally heard something I had been waiting to hear for six years. He told me that they wanted me to play in the big leagues! I started the season in AAA, in Indianapolis, and three weeks later, on May 8, 1989, I got called up. Now at last, I was in the big leagues."

My first pitching day was May 10, as a reliever. We had just come off a brawl after the seventh inning. I was nervous enough, but confident. We were winning 10–1, but the score didn't much matter. I pitched the ninth inning. I struck out the first guy up. The next batter grounded out. I was pretty pumped up. The next guy hit a double off me. I threw a bad pitch, and he hit it. I thought, Yeah, these are major league hitters — I'd better pay attention. Then I struck out the next batter to end the game. Well, I couldn't sleep at all that night. I was so excited, it was unbelievable.

"Gradually, I settled down. I realized it was going to be a different kind of year for me; I knew I wasn't going to get a lot of innings. I was the only rookie on a pitching staff of vets. We were trying to build a World Series team, we were ten games in first place. I was getting my outings here and there. I got my first major league win in front of my wife and family in Philadelphia. But we were in the dog days of August, and with September and a pennant race around the corner, my manager wasn't about to put the ball in a rookie's hands. My appearances were getting shorter, and I wasn't getting many innings. I ended up being 3–0, with some extra inning wins.

"I was feeling pretty good about myself, but the big shocker came when I got to New York. We were already losing when I gave up five runs in a single game. But then, two days later, when the manager had no choice but to put me into an extra inning game, I gave up a home run and we lost the game.

"I was sent down to Indianapolis, the AAA club, pitched really well, and we won the league and the alliance championships. I came home with a great positive attitude, and I worked very hard through the off-season. I played winter ball in Santo Domingo, in the Dominican Republic, mainly to get in as many innings as I could. We played in the Winter League world series, and I pitched well. I was a starter, so that I could get in as many innings as possible."

At the beginning of the 1991 season, Steve was slated to be the Expos' short left-handed reliever. "After a tough start, the Expos thought it would be best if I went down to get more innings at AAA camp. I spent three weeks in AAA and did well. So I went back up, but I didn't do so well, and I didn't pitch much. Then it was back to AAA, then back up to Montreal in September."

There's an old saying: as soon as you think you have the game of baseball beat, the game of baseball will beat you. Nothing just falls into place. "You have to work hard and maintain a good mental attitude — and never give up your dream!"

Lingo

Pan Am Games:
Amateur series of Olympic-type sporting events that are held in North or South America.

Sinker:
A type of pitch that drops into the strike zone suddenly as it reaches the plate. Now more likely called a slider, which is a faster pitch that does the same thing.

Change-up:
A type of pitch that is designed to throw off the hitter's timing. It can be a slow-breaking ball (in other words, a slow curveball or a slow screwball) or another type of pitch.

DL:
Disabled list. Players who are injured may be taken off the team's main roster and placed on an inactive list, called the DL. This allows the team to bring up a substitute player from the minor leagues without increasing the size of the team's roster.

Steve Frey: A Typical Day

A typical working day for a ballplayer begins in the middle of the afternoon and ends late at night. Steve usually gets up at about ten in the morning and eats a light breakfast of cereal and orange juice. After breakfast, Steve and his wife take care of family business or travel locally. "I try to do something enjoyable in the morning, nothing too exhausting." Facing a rigorous afternoon, Steve eats a big meal early in the afternoon. "I like to dig into carbohydrates like pasta, and I go easy on the red meats."

After the midday meal, Steve relaxes, allowing time to digest. He usually arrives at the ballpark before four for a seven-thirty game. "That's when I start my 'day at the office.' I check my mail — usually it's mostly fan mail — and then I change into my batting practice outfit. Before batting practice, some players do some extra work, like running or working with weights. During BP, I get some running in. When we're playing at home, pitchers take batting practice. After that, we have infield practice. A coach hits fly balls to the outfielders, and the pitchers relay the ball back to the coach."

Players take the forty-five minutes between practice and game time to change into game uniforms and relax. "Some guys get rubdowns. A lot of players have pre-game rituals. I like to do a few crossword puzzles to unwind." At 7:30, the whole team comes out for the national anthem. Since he is a late-inning reliever, Steve watches the game until the seventh inning, and then, if he's needed, he warms up. He exercises to stay limber, but he and his pitching coach are careful not to work his arm too hard in the bull pen.

Before every series, the team meets to talk about strategies. "Say we're playing the Phillies. We talk about how to pitch every player, what their strengths and weaknesses are." Players offer advice to one another both in this meeting and all through the series. "Everybody works as a team. If you're not winning, it's not a very good feeling. You pull for each other; you try to help each other out." In talking with another left-handed reliever, Steve might discuss the advantages of different angles for his throwing arm or different grips on a curveball. The pitching coach offers more specific advice. "He wants you to do well, because it's a reflection of his ability to teach you. A lot of pitching is mechanical, and the pitching coach keeps an eye on everything you do. Sometimes he concentrates on the mental side. They seem to know the right things to say."

Steve does not play every game, and when he does pitch, it's only for an inning or two at a time. "I'm so focused when I'm out there. The crowd noise is basically a buzz. If something exciting happens, you hear a big roar. My mind is really a blank. You don't want to try to think too much; you want your natural ability to take over. You got there basically on your ability, and if you think too much, you tend to make mistakes."

Pitchers depend heavily on their relationships with the team's catchers. "On and off the field, you try to have a good personal relationship with the catcher. When a catcher puts down that finger, you are trusting him to know the right pitch. Catchers are the ones you talk to a lot during batting practice and in the clubhouse. We talk about different strategies for different players. Should we stick with a particular pitch or try something different? By the time I get to that mound, the catcher and I have discussed the batters in detail, and we are in complete agreement about what we want to do.

"When you win, you feel good for yourself, but you also feel good for your team. It's hard to describe — baseball is such a team thing. Everyone really does work together toward a common goal: to win."

After the game, Steve ices his elbow and shoulder. "That's because your arm wasn't intended to throw a baseball ninety miles

Mid-reliever:
A relief pitcher who specializes in the middle innings of a game and usually replaces the starting pitcher. Also called a middle man.

Set-up Man:
A relief pitcher who specializes in following the mid-reliever but leaves the game prior to the closer — the relief pitcher who finishes the game.

an hour. That's why you get injuries. When you're out there throwing, the tendons in your elbows and shoulders get inflamed. You basically want to cool the arm down so that the arm rejuvenates quicker."

Win or lose, Steve is prepared for interviews following the game. "During the twenty minutes that I'm icing my arm, I do the interviews. The starters do the longer interviews. Reporters usually ask me about a particular pitch or how I felt at a particular moment, but it's usually very brief." Every year, the Expos hold a media workshop, a seminar for new players. Steve thinks this is useful: "You watch yourself being interviewed, and you learn to work with the media. After all, media can play a big role in your career."

As for statistics, "You do pay attention, but if you're pitching well, you don't have to look at the numbers to know that. A player's salary for the following year is based on statistics — won/lost, ERA, and in my case, the number of inherited runners and how many scored, and how I pitched to left-handed batters, which is really my job."

After the game, Steve meets his wife, who's usually waiting at the clubhouse door. He eats a light meal, more if he played that night. He leaves the stadium at about eleven, but he needs two or three hours to unwind. He tries to get to sleep by about two, allowing himself a full eight hours.

The schedule varies slightly for day games — he gets to the stadium earlier and goes home earlier, but the routine is about the same. When the team is away, wives and families don't travel with the team, but aside from some time in the morning to explore the city the team is visiting, his schedule does not vary.

Steve's ADVICE

"I think three things are the most important. The first is to set goals for yourself. The second is to stay away from drugs and live a clean life. And the third is to have fun."

When you're just starting out, maybe finishing with Little League and looking for more challenging competition, you should be playing the game because you enjoy it. It's fun to dream about someday becoming a professional ballplayer, but it's much too early to take that dream seriously.

By the time you're about fourteen or fifteen, it is vitally important that you stay out of trouble. You just don't want to hurt your chances, to develop any bad habits that might become problems later on. "It's good to set goals for yourself, and to give 100 percent of your energy to pursuing those goals, no matter what they might be. One goal might be to move up within your local team so that you're a starting pitcher. Once you make it to that goal, you might set another, that you're going to win three games in a row. When you prove to yourself that you can do that, you set another one, something that's harder to achieve. You will not satisfy every goal that you set for yourself — if you do, then the goals are too easy — but it's great to have something to strive for. And goal setting doesn't apply only to sports. You can also improve your performance at school by setting goals for yourself. This kind of training is really important. Even if you do make it into professional baseball, there are no guarantees. It's a business without much security, so a good education is important."

If your talents are strong, and you think you may eventually want to play professional ball, there are some steps you should take while you're a teenager. "You should be playing every day, if not at school then at a sports club, like the Police Athletic League. Since your skills and abilities are still forming, playing a variety of positions is better than concentrating on one or two at first. Listen to your coach; learn to trust him. The reason he got the coaching job is because he knows a lot about baseball. You can learn a lot by watching games on TV, and you can get videotapes for instruction. But don't stop with organized games and leagues. I played constantly with neighborhood kids. I think that's where you develop the real love of the game. When you're playing with friends, you're competing, but you're also having fun. Don't put any performance pressure on yourself. You are going to have your good days and your bad days. Even when you have a bad day, you'll probably learn something that will be helpful later on."

By your junior year in high school, you should focus on one or two, or maybe three, positions. "You may be working hard, but the emphasis should be on fun. Learn all that you can from your coach and from other players on the team. You can gain a lot by just listening and by watching other players in action. Your goals should be a little tougher, but again, it's best to avoid any serious performance pressure. If you're a pitcher, you might try to win ten games, for example."

The best players are likely to attract some attention from scouts. "A scout might ask you whether you're planning to go to college or whether you're willing to become a professional ballplayer. Some people don't want a career in sports — they're simply playing for fun. A scout doesn't want to recommend signing a player only to find out that he plans to go to med school and become a doctor. But the main reason they ask is to find out whether you'll be available right out of high school or whether you prefer to spend a few years in college first. If you're skilled, scouts will find out about you — you don't normally contact a scout directly."

When choosing a college, select one that offers both a strong baseball program and a solid academic reputation. "There are a lot of factors to consider. It's not as simple as saying that you want to go to a big college in the South that plays seventy-five games a year. You have to think about your family's financial situation. You have to consider your own academic record and whether you want a place that's close to home. A bigger school may have a better program, but you may be able to play more often at a smaller school. This is a decision that you should make with your family. If you're not sure whether college is for you, try a two-year school. For me, a junior college was the answer, and I signed after two years in school. There are plenty of junior colleges with strong baseball programs."

Many high school and college athletes are gifted, skillful, and perseverant. Only a small percentage are signed, and of those, an even smaller number get a chance on a major league team. "You must have the mental toughness, which you develop by setting and meeting goals. You've got to say to yourself, 'This is what I want to do' and work as hard as you can to make things happen. The harder I worked, the more I felt that things were happening for me."

If you are offered a professional contract, Steve encourages you to take it seriously. "Maybe thirty years from now, you'll be happy to know that you tried to take that shot to become a professional baseball player. If you don't do it, then thirty years from now, you could be saying to yourself, 'I could have done it, but I didn't.' I know a lot of people who dropped out early, and they'll never know what they could have done. I remember when I got to Oneonta and there were twenty pitchers on the field, I thought I'd never play at all. But I stayed with it, had fun, and took advantage of the situation. You'll never know what could happen unless you take the opportunities that are offered to you and make the best of them." ■

Where to Get More Information

BASEBALL TEAMS

MAJOR LEAGUES

The American League

The American Baseball League
350 Park Avenue
New York, NY 10022

Baltimore Orioles
Memorial Stadium
Baltimore, MD 21218

Boston Red Sox
Fenway Park
4 Yawkey Way
Boston, MA 02215

California Angels
P.O. Box 2000
Anaheim, CA 92806

Chicago White Sox
333 West 35th St.
Chicago, IL 60616

Cleveland Indians
Cleveland Stadium
Cleveland, OH 44114

Detroit Tigers
Tiger Stadium
Detroit, MI 48216

Kansas City Royals
P.O. Box 419969
Kansas City, MO 64141

Milwaukee Brewers
Milwaukee County Stadium
201 S. 46th St.
Milwaukee, WI 53214

Minnesota Twins
501 Chicago Ave. South
Minneapolis, MN 55415

New York Yankees
Bronx, NY 10451

Oakland Athletics
Oakland–Alameda County
  Coliseum
Oakland, CA 94621

Seattle Mariners
P.O. Box 4100
Seattle, WA 98104

Texas Rangers
P.O. Box 1111
Arlington, TX 76004

Toronto Blue Jays
Skydome
300 The Esplanade West
Box 3200
Toronto, Ontario
Canada M5V 3B3

The National League

The National Baseball League
350 Park Avenue
New York, NY 10022

Atlanta Braves
P.O. Box 4064
Atlanta, GA 30302

Chicago Cubs
Wrigley Field
1060 West Addison St.
Chicago, IL 60613

Cincinnati Reds
100 Riverfront Stadium
Cincinnati, OH 45202

Colorado Rockies
Suite 2100
1700 Broadway
Denver, CO 80290

Florida Marlins
100 NE Third Ave.
Ft. Lauderdale, FL 33301

Houston Astros
P.O. Box 288
Houston, TX 77001

Los Angeles Dodgers
Dodger Stadium
1000 Elysian Park Avenue
Los Angeles, CA 90012

Montreal Expos
P.O. Box 500, Station M
Montreal, Quebec
Canada H1V 3P2

New York Mets
Shea Stadium
126th St. and Roosevelt Ave.
Flushing, NY 11368

Philadelphia Phillies
P.O. Box 7575
Philadelphia, PA 19101

Pittsburgh Pirates
P.O. Box 7000
Pittsburgh, PA 15212

St. Louis Cardinals
250 Stadium Plaza
St. Louis, MO 63102

San Diego Padres
P.O. Box 2000
San Diego, CA 92120

San Francisco Giants
Candlestick Park
San Francisco, CA 94124

MINOR LEAGUES

National Association of Professional
    Baseball Leagues
P.O. Box A
St. Petersburg, FL 33731
Members include all minor leagues.

Class AAA Leagues

Triple-A Alliance
(includes International League and
American Association)

The Triple-A Alliance
3600 Broadway
P.O. Box 608
Grove City, OH 43123

Buffalo Bisons
P.O. Box 450
Buffalo, NY 14205

Columbus Clippers
1155 Mound St.
Columbus, OH 43223

Indianapolis Indians
1501 W. 16th St.
Indianapolis, IN 46202

Iowa Cubs
2nd & Riverside Dr.
Des Moines, IA 50309

Louisville Redbirds
Kentucky State Fairgrounds
Freedom Way and Phillips Lane
P.O. Box 36407
Louisville, KY 40223

Nashville Sounds
P.O. Box 23290
Nashville, TN 37202

Oklahoma City Eighty-Niners
All-Sports Stadium on the
   Fairgrounds
P.O. Box 75089
Oklahoma City, OK 73147

Omaha Royals
P.O. Box 3665
Omaha, NE 68103

Pawtucket Red Sox
P.O. Box 2365
Pawtucket, RI 02861

Richmond Braves
3001 North Blvd.
P.O. Box 6667
Richmond, VA 23230

Rochester Red Wings
500 Norton St.
Rochester, NY 14621

Scranton Red Barons
P.O. Box 3449
Scranton, PA 18505

Syracuse Chiefs
MacArthur Stadium
Syracuse, NY 13208

Tidewater Tides
6000 Northampton Blvd.
P.O. Box 12111
Norfolk, VA 23502

Toledo Mudhens
P.O. Box 6212
Toledo, OH 43614

Pacific Coast League

The Pacific Coast Baseball League
2101 East Broadway
Tempe, AZ 85282

Albuquerque Dukes
P.O. Box 26267
Albuquerque, NM 87125

Calgary Cannons
Foothills Baseball Stadium
Crowchild Trail and 24th Ave. NW
P.O. Box 3690, Station B
Calgary, Alberta
Canada T2M 4M4

Colorado Springs Sky Sox
4385 Tuft Blvd.
Colorado Springs, CO 80922

Edmonton Trappers
10233 96th Ave.
Edmonton, Alberta
Canada TK5 0A5

Las Vegas Stars
850 Las Vegas Blvd. N.
Las Vegas, NV 89101

Phoenix Firebirds
Phoenix Memorial Stadium
5999 E. Van Buren St.
Phoenix, AZ 85008

Portland Beavers
1844 SW Morrison Ave.
Portland, OR 97205

Tacoma Tigers
P.O. Box 11087
Tacoma, WA 98411

Tucson Toros
P.O. Box 27045
Tucson, AZ 85726

Vancouver Canadians
Nat Bailey Stadium
4601 Ontario St.
Vancouver, British Columbia
Canada V5V 3H4

Note: Minor league affiliations change periodically. For a complete, up-to-date list, contact each league office directly, or consult the latest Baseball America directory (see page 159).

Class AA Leagues

Eastern League
The Eastern Baseball League
P.O. Box 716
Plainfield, CT 06062
The Eastern League teams are located in Connecticut, New York, Ohio, Maryland, Pennsylvania, and Ontario (Canada).

Southern League
The Southern Baseball League
235 Main St., Suite 103
Trussville, AL 35173
The Southern League teams are located in Alabama, South Carolina, Tennessee, Georgia, and Florida.

Texas League
The Texas Baseball League
10201 W. Markham St., Suite 214
Little Rock, AR 72205
The Texas League teams are located in Arkansas, Texas, Mississippi, Louisiana, Kansas, and Oklahoma.

Class A Leagues

California League
The California Baseball League
1060 Willow St., P.O. Box 26400
San Jose, CA 95215
The California League teams are located in California and Nevada.

Carolina League
The Carolina Baseball League
P.O. Box 9503
Greensboro, NC 27429
The Carolina League teams are located in North Carolina, Maryland, and Virginia.

Florida State League
The Florida State Baseball League
P.O. Box 349
Daytona Beach, FL 32115
The Florida State League teams are located throughout the state.

Midwest League
The Midwest Baseball League
P.O. Box 936
Beloit, WI 53511
The Midwest League teams are located in Iowa, Indiana, Illinois, and Wisconsin.

South Atlantic League
The South Atlantic Baseball League
504 Crescent Hill
P.O. Box 38
King's Mountain, NC 28086
The South Atlantic League teams are located in North and South Carolina, Georgia, and West Virginia.

New York–Penn League
The New York–Penn Baseball League
P.O. Box 1313
Auburn, NY 13201
The New York–Penn League teams are located in Massachusetts, New York, Pennsylvania, and Ontario (Canada).

Northwest League
The Northwest Baseball League
P.O. Box 30025
Portland, OR 97230
The Northwest League teams are located in Oregon, Idaho, and Washington.

Rookie Leagues

The two largest rookie leagues are the Appalachian League (157 Carson Lane, Bristol, VA 24201), with teams in West Virginia, North Carolina, and Tennessee; and the Pioneer League (P.O. Box 1144, Billings, MT 59103), with teams in Montana, Idaho, Utah, and Alberta (Canada). Smaller rookie leagues include the Arizona League (P.O. Box 4941, Scottsdale, AZ 85261), the Gulf Coast League (1503 Clower Creek, Sarasota, FL 34231), and the Dominican Summer League (c/o Banco del Progreso, Av. John F. Kennedy, Santo Domingo, Dominican Republic).

BOOKS

The best source of information about baseball teams is *Baseball America's (Annual) Directory: The Complete Baseball Guide.* It's published by Baseball America (1-800-845-2726, outside North Carolina). You'll find it in most well-stocked bookstores. A companion volume, *Baseball America's (Annual) Almanac,* contains extensive information, including statistics, about major and minor league players.

Many books and essay collections have been published about players, teams, particular seasons, umpires, the baseball business, and so on. A new batch arrives every spring.

If you are serious about a career in baseball, you should learn about all aspects of the game — history, business, famous players, legendary teams, the roles that different professionals fill. Many of these books are written for adults, but most are not difficult reading.

Asinof, Elliot. *Eight Men Out.* New York: Henry Holt and Company, reprint 1977. The story of the 1919 Chicago Black Sox scandal, the basis for a motion picture of the same name (movie available on videocassette).

Gregg, Eric, and Marty Appel. *Working the Plate.* New York: William Morrow, 1990. An autobiography of umpire Eric Gregg.

Honig, Donald. *Baseball: The Illustrated History of America's Game.* New York: Crown, 1990. The best of several histories told through black-and-white pictures. Many such books are available; they're easy to find in public libraries.

Kahn, Roger. *The Boys of Summer.* New York: HarperCollins, 1971. The story of Jackie Robinson and the Brooklyn Dodgers, the first integrated team in major league baseball. (Documentary version available on home videocassette.)

Luciano, Ron, and David Fisher. *The Umpire Strikes Back.* New York: Bantam, 1984. Amusing backstage stories told by an outspoken major league umpire.

Peterson, R. *Only the Ball Was White: A History of Legendary Black Players and All-Black Professional Teams.* New York: McGraw-Hill, paperback 1984.

Ritter, Lawrence. *Glory of Their Times: The Story of the Early Days of Baseball Told by the Men Who Play.* New York: William Morrow, 1985. (Also available as a documentary on videocassette, though this tape can be hard to find.)

—————. *The Story of Baseball.* New York: Macmillan, 1982. A good condensed history written for young adults.

Sculley, Gerald. *The Business of Major League Baseball.* Chicago: University of Chicago Press, 1989. The best explanation of how the business works, from free agency to the ways in which teams make money. Unfortunately, it can be tough to read.

Seymour, Harold. *Baseball: The Early Years.* New York: Oxford University Press, 1960. *Baseball: The Golden Age.* New York: Oxford University Press, 1971. *Baseball: The People's Game.* New York: Oxford University Press, 1990. A three-volume history of the game, the fans, and the business of baseball.

Thorn, John, and Bob Carroll with David Reuther. *The Whole Baseball Catalog: The Ultimate Guide to the Baseball Marketplace.* New York: Fireside/Simon & Schuster, 1990. A vast collection of information about fantasy camps, baseball cards, songs about baseball, radio and television coverage, and dozens of other topics.

Whiting, Robert. *You Gotta Have Wa: When Two Cultures Collide on a Baseball Diamond.* New York: Vintage, 1990. Fascinating stories about players from the U.S. who have signed with teams in Japan.

Will, George F. *Men at Work: The Craft of Baseball.* New York: Macmillan, 1990.

And don't forget about the many biographies of famous baseball players and championship teams.

Most public libraries include several dozen books about baseball in their collections. You'll find a section of baseball books in most bookstores as well.

PERIODICALS

Extensive coverage of baseball is available in *USA Today,* local newspapers, and *Sporting News* (1212 N. Lindbergh Blvd., St. Louis, MO 63132), available on most newstands. *USA Today* also publishes *Baseball Weekly,* which includes stats, evaluations of players in the major and minor leagues, box scores, TV and radio schedules, and other essential information. *Sports Illustrated* is also essential reading, more for the overview than day-to-day coverage.

ARCHITECTURAL FIRMS

Several architectural firms specialize in baseball stadiums and sporting arenas. HOK (Hellmuth, Obata & Kassabaum, 323 West 8 Street, Kansas City, MO 64105) is the leading firm; recent projects include Pilot Field in Buffalo, New York, and the new Comiskey Park. Osborn Engineering's speciality is the restoration of older stadiums. Their address: 668 Euclid Avenue, Cleveland, OH 44144.

BASEBALL CAMPS

The best baseball camps provide concentrated, professional instruction to young athletes. Choose carefully, though, because these camps are costly and some are better than others.

Here are several names and addresses:

Bucky Dent's Baseball School
490 Dotterel Road
Delray Beach, FL 33444

Florida Professional Baseball School
P.O. Box 461
Snapper Creek, FL 33116

The Jim Rice Pro-Baseball Schools
P.O. Box 66479
St. Petersburg, FL 33706

Mickey Owen Baseball School
P.O. Box 88
Miller, MO 65707

"Play Ball" Baseball Academy
P.O. Box 48558
Ft. Lauderdale, FL 33338
(also holds summer classes on Cape Cod, Massachusetts)

Jack Aker Baseball
P.O. Box 1222
Port Washington, NY 11050

San Diego School of Baseball
4688 Alvarado Canyon Road
Suite Q
San Diego, CA 92120

OTHER ADDRESSES OF INTEREST

Association of Professional Baseball
  Physicians (APBP)
606 24th Ave. South
Minneapolis, MN 55454

National Baseball Hall of Fame and
  Library
P.O. Box 590
Cooperstown, NY 13326

Major League Scouting Bureau
23712 Birtcher Dr.
El Toro, CA 92630

Major League Baseball Umpire
  Development
201 Bayshore Dr. SE
St. Petersburg, FL 33701

THE WINTER MEETING

Every December, front office people from the major and minor leagues get together for a convention called the winter meeting. Usually held in a warm location such as Florida or Arizona, the meeting is actually a series of seminars and workshops. Representatives from every team usually go to the winter meeting with plans to interview job candidates. For this reason, attending the winter meeting is a good idea, particularly when you're starting out and you need to make contacts. The winter meeting is a professional gathering, and it is wise to attend only when you are ready to start working full-time.

The best way to plan for the winter meeting is as follows. First, during the summer, contact the baseball commissioner's office (Major League Baseball, Office of the Commissioner, 350 Park Avenue, New York, NY 10022) to find out where the meeting will be held. Second, make a hotel reservation — hotels fill up early. Third, decide which teams you would like to work for. Write a letter to the appropriate person from each team (these names can be found in each team's media guide, available for a few dollars; media guides can be ordered by mail or purchased at ballparks). Let the person know that you will attend the winter meeting, and try to set up an appointment. Fourth, prepare your resume and any other background information, and make at least a hundred copies — you will want to have enough for anyone who asks. Fifth, look your best — dress professionally; look like someone who can do the job. Sixth, go the meetings and be aggressive (but not too aggressive) — be sure you know who you want to see, track down each person over the days of the meeting, and be prepared to show yourself in the best possible light. Many other people will be doing the same, and there will be competition. But there will also be a few dozen jobs available for the right candidates — if you're well dressed, prepared, and capable, your odds are improved considerably.